CHALLENGES OF VIOLENCE WORLDWIDE

A CURRICULUM MODULE

CHALLENGES OF VIOLENCE WORLDWIDE

A CURRICULUM MODULE

Written and Compiled by
Dorothy Van Soest and Jane Crosby
For the Violence & Development Project

NASW PRESS

National Association of Social Workers
Washington, DC

Jay J. Cayner, ACSW, LSW, *President*
Josephine Nieves, MSW, PhD, *Executive Director*

Linda Beebe, *Executive Editor*
Nancy A. Winchester, *Editorial Services Director*
Wendy Almeleh, *Copy Editor*
Louise Goines, *Proofreader*
Patricia D. Wolf, Wolf Publications, Inc., *Proofreader*
Angland Creek Indexing, *Indexer*

The six parts in this educational resource were developed with the assistance of six NASW chapter-based Violence and Development Project Centers and a Curriculum Development Working Group of the Council on Social Work Education's International Commission.

This publication was made possible through support provided by a Development Education matching grant, number FAO-0230-A-00-3041-00, from the Office of Private and Voluntary Cooperation, Bureau for Food and Humanitarian Assistance, U.S. Agency for International Development. The views expressed herein do not necessarily reflect those of USAID.

Library of Congress Cataloging-in-Publication Data
Van Soest, Dorothy
    Challenges of violence worldwide : a curriculum module / written
and compiled by Dorothy Van Soest and Jane Crosby.
        p.   cm.
    "For the Violence & Development Project."
    "Intended for use with the accompanying Challenges of violence
worldwide : an educational resource (student version)"—P. 1.
    Includes bibliographical references and index.
    ISBN 0-87101-268-5 (alk. paper)
    1. Violence—Study and teaching (Higher)   2. Social problems—
Study and teaching (Higher)   3. Social policy—Study and teaching
(Higher)   4. Social work education.   I. Crosby, Jane.   II. Title.
HM281.V29   1996
303.6'071'1—dc21   96-29539
                                                                            CIP

Printed in the United States of America

Dedicated to Eileen McGowan Kelly
for her consistent and visionary leadership
in advancing the international dimensions of social work

CONTENTS

PART 3   47

VIOLENCE AGAINST WOMEN AND CHILDREN: BEYOND A FAMILY AFFAIR

PART 4   65

ETHNICITY:
A RICH, DIVERSE WORLD

PART 5   85

DRUG ABUSE:
ENDING THE GLOBAL EPIDEMIC

PART 6   **103**

TRAUMA:
SURVIVAL IS VICTORY

PREFACE

In 1980, President Carter's Commission on Hunger found that the American public knew very little about the extent of hunger and poverty in the rest of the world. This ignorance exists despite the fact that the problem is so pervasive. Although things have steadily improved in many regions, 1.1 billion of the world's people still live in poverty. Eight hundred million are chronically hungry.

As a result of the findings of the commission, the U.S. Congress passed a law that sets aside money for programs to educate Americans about the challenges facing underdeveloped countries and efforts being made to improve living standards there.

The National Association of Social Workers (NASW), through its Peace and International Affairs program, received some of this funding in 1988 when it was awarded its first development education grant from the United States Agency for International Development (USAID). Building on five years of experience, NASW received its third USAID grant in 1993. The initiative that was subsequently launched is called the Violence and Development Project. The *Educational Resource* and *Curriculum Module* that you hold in your hands are one result of this initiative.

The main objective of the project has been to expand the context within which social workers address social problems to include a global understanding of the relationship between violence and development. Six NASW chapter-based project centers, involving 11 states, were established as part of the project. The centers engaged the talents of hundreds of their chapter members at the grassroots level in developing educational materials, educating their constituents locally and regionally on violence and development issues, and organizing teach-in activities. The project centers were the Northwest Center on Violence, Development, and Ethnicity (involving the Oregon, Idaho, and Washington NASW chapters); the New York City NASW chapter Center on Violence, Development, and Poverty; the

California NASW chapter Center on Violence, Development, and Trauma; the Florida NASW chapter Center on Violence, Development, and Trauma; the Minnesota NASW chapter Center on Violence, Development, and Women and Children; and the Midwest Center on Violence, Development, and Substance Abuse (involving the Michigan, Ohio, Illinois, and Indiana NASW chapters).

A highlight of the project came in February 1996, when a national Teach-In titled *Social Workers and the Challenge of Violence Worldwide* was held on the campuses of several hundred schools of social work in 41 states, Puerto Rico, and the Virgin Islands. Local organizers put together programs about violence and development. Two landmark national satellite video conferences were broadcast live during the week. Both programs were moderated by renowned CBS broadcast journalist Charles Kuralt. Twenty thousand social workers watched. During the second broadcast, viewers around the country interacted live via telephone with Mr. Kuralt and a panel of speakers.

From the experience of the Teach-In week, we learned that social workers are eager to study community building and global learning as a response to violence. Ninety percent of those who responded to a national evaluation felt that these topics should be incorporated into social work training at every level.

The *Educational Resource* and *Curriculum Module* are one response to this need for training. For topics as enormous as development, violence, and global interdependence, no one book contains all the answers. But these materials do represent one more step forward in the efforts of social workers to better understand and respond to a rapidly changing world. It is our hope that they will help social workers see their profession in an international context and understand that countries in the developing world, while struggling with issues and problems similar to our own, have created models and approaches that can be useful to us.

Dorothy Van Soest and Jane Crosby
August 1996

ACKNOWLEDGMENTS

The Violence and Development Project, out of which this resource evolved, is a truly collaborative one, and literally hundreds of people have been involved in shaping it.

Volunteers were the mainstay of the project. The International Activities and the Peace and Justice Committees of the National Association of Social Workers have long been dedicated to the issues addressed in these materials, and their previous efforts provided the foundation on which this work was built. A national advisory committee to the project gave more time and expertise than was ever expected through active participation in all phases of the work.

Hundreds of volunteer NASW members contributed through six chapter-based project centers in 11 states. The Council on Social Work Education (CSWE) was a collaborating organization in this project, with dedicated members of the International Commission making valuable contributions. We extend a special thanks to Sally Van der Straeten and Yvonne Asamoah. Although it is impossible to name everyone who contributed, individuals from the project centers and the CSWE Curriculum Development Working Group deserve special recognition: Joe Gallegos, Marie Hoff, Janet Kusyk, Jennifer Stucker, and Daniel Tovar (Northwest Center on Violence, Development, and Ethnicity); Marilynn Moch and Beth S. Rosenthal (New York City NASW chapter Center on Violence, Development, and Poverty); Gerald Gray, Arleen B. Kahn, Mary Mussell, Arline Prigoff, and Krishna Samantrai (California NASW chapter Center on Violence, Development, and Trauma); Charles Figley, Kenneth Kazmerski, and Linda Vinton (Florida NASW chapter Center on Violence, Development, and Trauma); Bruce Ellsworth, Allie Kilpatrick, Pat Leahan, Rosemary Link, Rosemarie Merrigan, and Maura Sullivan (Minnesota NASW chapter Center on Violence, Development, and Women and Children); Shantha Balaswamy, James O. Billups, Lorraine Blackman, Debbie Ruboyianes, JoAnne St. Clair, Judy Smith, Chathapuram Ramanthan, and Jack Wall (Midwest Center on Violence, Development, and Substance Abuse).

The Alliance for a Global Community/Inter-Action provided critical information and expertise all along the way, always with a generous and enthusiastic response. A special thanks to Janet Green.

This project was funded in part by the U.S. Agency for International Development. Without their support, and that of their dedicated program officers, this project would not have happened. To Susan Saragi, in particular, thanks for helping us with all the details, large and small. David Watson and Elise Storck served as outstanding project officers, providing guidance and support at all phases of our work.

Lucy Sanchez was there from the beginning— helping to develop the grant proposal and shaping the project design. She continued to be at the forefront of the project through all its phases.

As national outreach coordinator, Bob Lagoyda provided an undying commitment and endless good ideas. John Rice gave heart and soul to the project as a social work intern at the NASW national office.

Gratitude goes to Brenda Ruiz-Bustos and Esperanca Cardoso for all the work they have done to ensure the success of the project and these materials.

Special thanks to Cheryl White for her hard work as a contributing editor for the briefing papers that formed the basis for the *Educational Resource*. Special thanks also to the development education consultants from the Development Studies Program for sharing their expertise with us: Margee Ensign, Ken Kusterer, and Sam Samarasinghe.

David Weiner and Paul Aaron of the Benton Foundation have been true partners in this endeavor and their guidance has been invaluable. The mission of the Benton Foundation is to strengthen the communications capacities of nonprofit organizations.

Linda Beebe, associate executive director, communications, at NASW, was instrumental in organizing these guides. Nancy Winchester, editorial services director, expedited the production process. Freelance editors Wendy Almeleh and Louise Goines edited and refined the text. To all of them, our thanks.

And finally, our greatest appreciation to Eileen Kelly, who founded the Peace and International Affairs Program at NASW nine years ago. Her unending good humor has made this adventure a joy.

Dorothy Van Soest and Jane Crosby

PART I

CHAPTER 1-1

OVERVIEW

CURRICULUM

As noted in the Council on Social Work Education's 1994 *Handbook on Accreditation Standards and Procedures*, effective social work education programs recognize the interdependence of nations and the need for worldwide professional cooperation. *Challenges of Violence Worldwide: A Curriculum Module* focuses on violence as a global affliction and sustainable human development as a powerful avenue to intervention. The aim of this module is to contribute to the inclusion of more global content in social work education and to stimulate further curriculum development.

This module is intended for use with the accompanying *Challenges of Violence Worldwide: An Educational Resource* (student version) as assigned reading for any social work foundation course at either the bachelor's or master's degree level. *An Educational Resource* contains information and case studies on six topics: overview (an introduction to general concepts and to the linkages between violence and development), poverty, women and children, ethnicity, drug abuse, and trauma.

The *Curriculum Module* includes course objectives, discussion questions, and various class activities and course assignments. For the convenience of faculty, it also includes the full text of *An Educational Resource*. Course objectives for different parts of the curriculum have been suggested in the hope that faculty will add at least one global objective to syllabi for all of their courses.

GENERAL OBJECTIVES

1. Students will be able to describe parallel conditions of violence in the United States and in less economically advantaged nations.
2. Students will demonstrate a broadened understanding of violence and the role of the social work profession in solving the problem on a global scale.
3. Students will demonstrate an increased interest in learning from successful interventions by human services workers in developing countries and in the United States.
4. Students will be able to define key concepts, such as sustainable human development, global North, and global South.
5. Students will demonstrate an awareness of social work's commitment to social justice by describing how violence and oppression affect vulnerable populations throughout the world.

The objectives and discussion questions in the following section are presented by curriculum area. The questions may be used for classroom discussion or in written assignments. They are based on information presented in part 1 of *An Educational Resource* (pp. 15 to 21 in this volume and pp. 1 to 7 in the student version).

HUMAN BEHAVIOR IN THE SOCIAL ENVIRONMENT

Objectives

1. Students will demonstrate an understanding of the impact of personal, institutional, and structural violence on the development of individuals and families throughout the life cycle and on the social and economic development of communities and societies.
2. Students will demonstrate an understanding of the parallel conditions of violence and the impact of violence on individuals and communities in both the United States and in less economically developed countries.
3. Students will begin to identify how social workers can intervene with social systems and demand social justice for the benefit of human growth and development worldwide.

Discussion Questions

1. How do you define violence? What are some implications of the broadened definition of violence presented in part 1 of *An Educational Resource* (p. 16 in this volume and p. 2 in the student version) for individual and social development?
2. Can you provide at least one example of a form of violence at each of the three levels—personal, institutional, and structural—and discuss the impact of such violence on individual development across the life span. (See part 1 of An Educational *Resource*—p. 17 in this volume and p. 3 in the student version—for a description of the three levels of violence.)
3. What are some parallels between the United States and countries of the global South in relation to the impact of violence on individual and social development? How do you define development?

SOCIAL WORK THEORY AND PRACTICE

Objectives

1. Students will demonstrate an understanding of the connection between their clients' well-being and the political, social, and economic context within which their clients live.
2. Students will expand their definition of practice interventions to include such strategies as those aimed at reducing gun violence and militarization.
3. Students will be able to describe conflict-resolution strategies for use with individuals, families, and communities as an alternative to violence.

Discussion Questions

1. What are the implications of the broadened definition of violence in part 1 of *An Educational Resource* (pp. 16–17 in this volume and pp. 2–3 in the student version) for social work interventions?
2. What is the relevance of the concept of sustainable human development for social work intervention in the United States? Discuss the similar and different uses of such a strategy in the United States and in the global South.
3. What knowledge and skills does the social work profession offer to international efforts to promote global security and development? What further knowledge and skills does the profession need to develop?

SOCIAL WELFARE POLICY

Objectives

1. Students will be able to describe the connections among different forms of violence and the obstruction of the processes of individual, social, and economic development.
2. Students will be able to explain the ways in which social work support for human and economic development efforts in the global South are linked with social work concerns about violence in the United States.
3. Students will be able to discuss the significant links between U.S. foreign policy and U.S. social welfare policy and examine ways in which attitudes about violence and militarism influence the political debate about social issues.

Discussion Questions

1. What relevance do the principles underlying sustainable human development have for social welfare policy and practice?
2. Domestic social welfare policy is concerned with poverty and inequity in the United States. Should social workers in the United States also be concerned with inequities between the global North and the global South? Why or why not?
3. Should domestic social welfare policy be concerned with U.S. foreign and military policies? Why or why not?

RESEARCH

Objectives

1. Students will develop an awareness of how research on violence and development issues from a global perspective relates to social work practice and policy.
2. Students will gain an understanding, based on research, of the impact of violence on human, social, and economic development.
3. Students will become familiar with the multidisciplinary research literature on international development.

Discussion Questions

1. How can research skills and information gained from research be used to learn more about the possible relationships between violence and development related to the social and economic growth of communities and countries?
2. How does the research literature define violence? Is there a standard social science definition? What are the implications of the broadened definition provided in *An Educational Resource* for research studies?

FIELD PRACTICUM

Objectives

1. Students will acquire a greater understanding of and commitment to the roles of social

workers within a global perspective.
2. Students will demonstrate a willingness to learn from successful projects in less economically developed countries.
3. Students will be able to describe specific development projects that have been successful in alleviating social problems in the global South and have been replicated in underdeveloped areas in the United States.

Discussion Questions

1. What is the relevance of violence and development issues in the global South for social work practice in your field placement in regard to the prevention and amelioration of violence?
2. How can you use the concept of sustainable human development in your field placement?

Exercise 1—Videotape
Social Workers and the Challenge of Violence Worldwide

Purpose

To introduce students to the connections between violence and development and motivate them to learn more.

Learning Activity

Show part 1 of the nationwide video conference, *Social Workers and the Challenge of Violence Worldwide*, which was hosted by Charles Kuralt and produced by the National Association of Social Workers. The one-hour videotape can be purchased from the NASW Press.

Introduce the videotape of part 1 by telling students that it was produced in February 1996 and that 20,000 social work students, faculty, and practitioners across the United States viewed it as part of a nationwide week-long teach-in. Part 1 consists of (1) a panel presentation–discussion and video segments in which the concept of development is defined and illustrated, (2) a discussion of violence as the enemy of the community and community development, and (3) hope for social change. After you show the videotape, have the students discuss the following questions.

Discussion Questions

1. What were your general impressions while viewing the videoconference?
2. What struck you the most about the presentation? What aspects were the most informative?
3. What were the primary messages?
4. What are the implications of what you learned for you as a social worker?

The videotape of part 2 of the videoconference includes a panel of social workers interacting with students, faculty, and practitioners via telephone about violence and development issues; it can also be purchased from NASW Press.

Exercise 2—Research Assignment
Learning about the Refugees in Your Community

Purpose

To obtain information about the refugees in the local community and the implications of that information for the delivery of social services.

Learning Activity

Have the students conduct research about a refugee population in the local community as a group assignment. The research should cover the following areas:

- a social history of the refugee group, including conditions in country of origin and reasons for coming to the United States
- the role and effects of violence (physical and structural) in the lives of individuals in the group
- cultural norms, traditions, and beliefs
- current needs and available services
- services that are needed and needs that are not met
- implications for social work practice.

Product

A group paper presenting the results of the research or a group presentation (or both) is suggested.

Source: Van Soest, 1992, p. 52.

Exercise 3—Class Discussion
The Global South Is Where . . .

Purpose

To build awareness of the characteristics of the global South and why this area of the world matters to social workers in the United States.

Introduction

The term *global South* refers to the world's poor nations, in contrast to the *global North*, which refers to wealthy, industrialized countries like the United States. In addition, U.S. social workers have traditionally been concerned about poor communities that are hidden in urban centers or isolated rural areas of this country.

Underdeveloped areas of the United States and countries of the global South share many characteristics, such as low standards of living, malnutrition, disease, illiteracy, unemployment, and inadequate or nonexistent medical services. In spite of parallel conditions, social workers in general tend not to be aware of or have information about the global South and have given little thought to its relevance for them and their clients.

Process

Have the students read "The global South is where . . ." (p. 16 of part 1 of *An Educational Resource* in this volume and p. 2 in the student version) and discuss the following questions either in small groups or in the class as a whole.

Discussion Questions

1. Which characteristics of the global South surprised you?
2. What are the differences between the characteristics of the global South and those of poor communities in the United States? What are the similarities?
3. Why should social workers have a global perspective?
4. What are the pros and cons of U.S. social workers supporting human and economic development efforts aimed at changing the characteristics of the global South?
5. What are the dilemmas inherent in the social work profession supporting such efforts?
6. What are some things that individual social workers and the profession as a whole can do to change some of the characteristics of the global South and the parallel conditions in underdeveloped regions of the United States?

Exercise 4—Questions and Answers
To Test Student Knowledge of International Development

Purpose

To increase knowledge about international development and the U.S. policy on foreign assistance and aid to countries of the global South.
Introduction

Perhaps one of the most often-asked questions today is, "Why, when we have so many problems at home, are we sending money to other countries?" The debate by both houses of Congress and the American public over the merits of helping other countries and the expense of doing so versus the use of funds to help solve problems in this country is fraught with stereotypes, misperceptions, and misinformation. In addition, there is little understanding of the concept of global interdependence and the reality that assistance to other countries is as important to the United States as it is to countries in the global South. This exercise is intended to dispel some myths and increase students' understanding of the connections between domestic and foreign policy.

Process

Have the students complete the worksheet, "20 True–False Questions to Test Your Knowledge of International Development." Then, go over the answers on the handout with them and discuss the issues presented in the following questions.

Discussion Questions

1. What is the most significant thing you learned from this exercise?
2. What are the implications of U.S. foreign policy for U.S. social welfare policy?
3. Do you think it is important for U.S. social workers to be informed about the global South? If so, why? If not, why not?

20 TRUE–FALSE QUESTIONS TO TEST YOUR KNOWLEDGE OF INTERNATIONAL DEVELOPMENT

T F

1. There are more nations in the global South (poor nations) than nations in the global North (wealthy industrialized nations).

T F

2. Life expectancy at birth is on the decline in the global South.

T F

3. English is the first language of a greater number of people in the world than any other language.

T F

4. Poverty is the basic cause of hunger today.

T F

5. About 5 percent of the world's population go hungry every day.

T F

6. Only a small percentage of U.S. trade is with countries in the global South.

T F

7. Most of the world's population live in the global South.

T F

8. More people live in Asia than in any other region of the world.

T F

9. Poor nutrition and inadequate health care are the leading causes of sickness and death in the world.

T F

10. The majority of cases of blindness are in the global North.

T F

11. Drinking and bathing account for more than 50 percent of the fresh water used throughout the world.

T F

12. The majority of people over age 60 in the world live in the industrialized countries of the global North.

T F

13. The three largest markets for U.S. goods are countries in the global North.

T F

14. About 90 percent of the growth in the world's population by the year 2002 will take place in the global South.

T F

15. Official development assistance accounts for about 10 percent of the U.S. gross national product (GNP).

T F

16. The United States allocates more of its GNP to foreign assistance than it does to welfare expenditures in the United States.

T F

17. The World Bank and the International Monetary Fund are the primary U.S. agencies that facilitate U.S. development assistance to the global South.

T F

18. The percentage of children age 15 and younger is much greater in the global South than in the global North.

T F

19. The United States is the most generous foreign assistance donor in the world.

T F

20. Most U.S. foreign aid dollars are spent in the United States.

Source: Adapted with permission from Kerschner, H. K. (1992). An organizing guide for community-based education and international action (p. 15). Washington, DC: American Association for International Aging.

This worksheet may be photocopied for classroom use.

1. **True.**

   The World Bank classifies 79 countries as "developing economies," or countries in the global South. Another 42 countries are generally identified as "developed" countries, or countries in the global North.

2. **False.**

   Life expectancy at birth in developing countries of the global South is expected to increase from 46 years in 1960 to 70 years by 2020.

3. **False.**

   English is the first language of about 420 million people, whereas Mandarin Chinese is spoken by about 788 million people.

4. **True.**

   Except for those living in food-emergency areas, most of the hungry people in the world are hungry because they are poor people living in areas where they have little opportunity to improve their incomes and hence to obtain sufficient food.

5. **False.**

   The World Bank estimated that about 20 percent of the world's people suffer from chronic undernourishment. Of those who are hungry, 75 percent live in India, Southeast Asia, and Sub-Saharan Africa.

6. **False.**

   In the 1980s, two-fifths of U.S. exports were purchased by countries of the global South. From 1985 to 1995, U.S. exports to developing countries more than doubled—from $71 billion to $180 billion.

7. **True.**

   In 1980, 74 percent of the world's 4.5 billion people lived in the global South. By the year 2000, when the world's population is expected to reach 6.1 billion, 79 percent will live in the global South. The world's population is expected to reach 10 billion by 2040.

8. **True.**

   Asia is the largest region with the largest population and the greatest diversity in geography and climate. About 25 percent of the people live in cities. There is only half an arable acre for each person. Life expectancy at birth is only 58 years. The population of the continent is expected to double by the year 2030.

9. **False.**

   The World Health Organization estimated that 80 percent of all sickness and diseases in the world are attributable to impure water or the lack of sanitation. These illnesses include the effects of drinking contaminated water, contact with water that is a breeding ground for germs and other carriers of disease, and diseases caused by the lack of washing.

10. **False.**

    According to the National Council on International Health, more than 80 percent of all blind people live in the global South, and fully two-thirds of all blindness is preventable, surgically reversible, or surgically arrestable.

11. **False.**

    Agriculture accounts for 70 percent of the world's use of fresh water.

12. **False.**

    In 1980 it was estimated that 53 percent of the population age 60 or over lived in the global South; that percentage is expected to increase to 69 percent by the year 2020.

13. **False.**

    Mexico, which is in the global South, is the third largest market for U.S. goods, behind Canada and Japan. It is also the United States's fourth largest market for agricultural products.

14. **True.**

The population of the countries that are now classified as being part of the global South is projected to grow from 3.32 billion in 1980 to 4.86 billion in 2000—an increase of 1.5 billion, or 92 percent of the world's projected growth. During that period, the population of countries of the global North is projected to grow from 1.14 billion to 1.28 billion—an increase of only 139.7 million.

15. **False**.

Official development assistance accounts for less than 1 percent of the U.S. GNP, which makes the United States 21st among countries in giving aid.

16. **False.**

Welfare constituted only 1 percent of the federal budget in 1992 and foreign aid even less.

17. **False.**

The U.S. Agency for International Development is the primary U.S. agency responsible for providing development assistance to the global South. The International Monetary Fund and the World Bank are multilateral development organizations supported by more than 150 countries, including the United States.

18. **True.**

Individuals age 15 years or younger constitute about 35 percent of the population in the global South, but only 21 percent of the population of the United States and Canada. The world's pool of potential child workers has nearly doubled since 1950. In 1987 it was estimated that 88 million children age 11 to 15 worked for a living.

19. **False.**

The United States is now fourth behind Japan, France, and Germany as the largest donor of official development assistance (in dollars), but, as a percentage of the GNP contributed, it is 21st behind Norway, Denmark, Sweden, Netherlands, France, Canada, Luxembourg, Switzerland, Australia, Portugal, Germany, Austria, Belgium, Finland, the United Kingdom, Japan, Spain, Italy, Ireland, and New Zealand.

20. **True.**

It is estimated that more than half the U.S. foreign aid dollars are spent in the United States on goods and services provided to countries of the global South.

Source: Adapted with permission from Kerschner, H.K. (1992). An organizing guide for community-based education and international action (pp. 48–49). Washington, DC: American Association for International Aging.

Exercise 5—Writing Assignment
Critical Evaluation of the News Media's Coverage of a Global Issue

Purpose

To help students become critical thinkers and consumers of information related to international issues of significance to social workers.

Learning Activity

Have the students find two or more articles, editorials, or speeches that present different views of the same issue or event. The sources should reflect different political and ideological perspectives, for example, an article from *The Nation* and an article from the *National Review*.

Some issues that you may want to suggest for this assignment are immigration and refugee policy; working conditions of migrant workers; international border issues; the North American Free Trade Agreement (NAFTA); any international conference, such as the Fourth World Conference on Women, held in Beijing in 1995; an ethnic conflict; or nuclear proliferation treaties or issues of nuclear testing.

The students should analyze the two articles, paying particular attention to
1. distinguishing between fact and opinion
2. identifying evidence of bias (sexual, racial, ethnic, political, or religious)
3. summarizing the authors' points of view and considering, to the extent possible, what in their life situations may predispose the authors to have taken these positions
4. analyzing assumptions that indicate a particular worldview or ideological perspective
5. identifying additional information that lead one to understand the particular issue or event more thoroughly
6. deciding which position or synthesis of positions or even an entirely different position the student would take and its "goodness of fit" for social work.

Remind the students that both facts and opinions are important and should be communicated, but that it is essential for them to understand the difference and to evaluate the information accordingly.

Paper

The paper should be typed double-spaced and accompanied by photocopies of the material being analyzed. It should cover the foregoing six points.

This assignment was adapted from an assignment developed by Professor Lois Martin for the course, "Social Policy and Social Justice: Global Perspectives on Social Welfare," presented at Salem State College, Salem, Massachusetts. Other issues and topics that are relevant for courses on human behavior in the social environment or social work practice or that can be adapted to courses on research can also be selected.

Source: Van Soest, 1992, p. 99.

Exercise 6—Pro and Con Position Paper

Purpose

To develop skills in analyzing a perspective, developing a position about it, and convincing others about the need to take action.

Learning Activity

Each student will write a position paper that consists of scholarly, well-reasoned arguments "for" a particular point of view (or "against" a point of view). This is intended to be a mind-stretching exercise, based on the idea that one of the best ways to analyze a point of view (an ideological position, a policy, a course of action, and so forth) is to argue the best "case" for it. Remind the students that issues of concern to social workers are not always clear and that areas of ambiguity often predominate, but that social workers must often take positions.

In this assignment, each student will take a specific position; write a paper in which he or she tries to convince someone, in a scholarly and reflective way, about the necessity of a particular course of action; and present the paper to the class. Remind the students that the assignment is not intended to be a debate but a scholarly presentation. The students may wish to define the audience they are trying to convince (such as a co-worker, supervisor, legislator, or member of a professional committee).

Possible Topics

Students should choose one of the following topics or negotiate a topic with the instructor.

1. The social work profession should advocate for
   a. domestic social welfare policies only
   b. both domestic and foreign policy issues.
2. The United States should solve its own social problems before it addresses those of less economically developed countries: yes or no.
3. Social workers who are therapists or case managers do not need to have a global perspective: yes or no.
4. Federal spending priorities should be weighted in favor of domestic programs rather than military programs: yes or no.
5. Social workers in the United States can learn much from their colleagues in less economically developed countries and apply what they have learned to practice in the United States: yes or no.
6. Social work support for human and economic development efforts around the world is actually a part of an overall program for addressing domestic issues: yes or no.
7. Federal expenditures for foreign assistance should be reduced: yes or no.
8. With all the violence in the world today, it is clear that people are instinctively and naturally prone to violence: yes or no.
9. When working with refugees, social workers should focus on the refugees' new life in the United States by addressing present and future needs, rather than attending to issues from the past: yes or no.

Written Paper

The paper should include the following:
- a clear statement of purpose, including the topic that the student is arguing for or against, how the argument will be made, and a summary of the student's reasons for his or her position
- definitions of key terms or concepts that are relevant to the topic

- a comparative and international perspective and references to the experiences of one or more other countries
- a conclusion, in which the points are summarized and integrated, and the argument is related to the larger picture, so that the reader understands what it all means
- a reference section, with complete references presented in the style of the fourth edition of the *Publication Manual of the American Psychological Association* (1994), keyed to name/date citations in the text.

Oral Presentation

Each student should be given 15 minutes to present his or her position to the class. Because the purpose is to convince the audience of a position, the student should refer to the paper while presenting the oral argument but not read it. Tell the students that they can use whatever supportive materials they think would help, such as audiovisual aids and bibliographies, and that they should pay attention to their delivery, start from the understanding that their intended audience already has, and provide interesting and convincing information.

This assignment was adapted from an assignment developed by Professor Thomas Watts for the course, "Foundations of Social Welfare Policy and Services," at the University of Texas at Arlington. It can also be used in courses on human behavior in the social environment or social work practice and can be adapted to courses on research.

Source: Van Soest, 1992, pp. 106–107.

REFERENCES

American Psychological Association. (1994). *Publication manual of the American Psychological Association* (4th ed.). Washington, DC: Author.

Council on Social Work Education. (1994). *Handbook on accreditation standards and procedures.* Alexandria, VA: Author.

InterAction. (1996). *How much of the federal budget is spent on foreign aid?* Washington, DC: Author. (InterAction, 1717 Massacusetts Avenue, NW, Washington, DC 20036; phone 202-667-8227)

Van Soest, D. (1992). *Incorporating peace and social justice into the social work curriculum.* Washington, DC: National Association of Social Workers, Office of Peace and International Affairs.

FOR FURTHER READING

Estes, R. J. (Ed.). (1992). *Internationalizing social work education: A guide to resources for a new century.* Philadelphia: University of Pennsylvania School of Social Work.
This book provides a wealth of resources that address a variety of international-development topics that are of interest to social work.

Healy, L. (1992). *Introducing international development content in the social work curriculum.* Washington, DC: National Association of Social Workers, Office of Peace and International Affairs.

This book presents key concepts, curriculum issues, and learning modules on global poverty, hunger and development, the rights of children, and intercountry adoption as a field of application.

Hokenstad, M. C., Khinduka, S. K., & Midgley, J. (1992). *Profiles in international social work.* Washington, DC: NASW Press.

This book examines international social work and its growing implications in an increasingly interdependent world and presents case studies of social work in 13 politically and socially diverse nations.

Van Soest, D. (1992). *Incorporating peace and social justice into the social work curriculum.* Washington, DC: National Association of Social Workers, Office of Peace and International Affairs.

This curriculum resource, based on a broadened definition of violence and written from a global perspective, presents information, course objectives, class assignments and exercises, audiovisual resources, and a bibliography in five social work foundation areas (Human Behavior in the Social Environment, Theory and Practice, Social Welfare Policy, Research, and Field Practicum).

CHAPTER 1-2

OVERVIEW

EDUCATIONAL RESOURCE

From the Los Angeles teenager whose friend is shot dead to the New York City executive who is mugged on a street corner, from the infant in Bombay who suffers from hunger to the poor farmer fleeing civil war in Rwanda, violence affects millions of people worldwide. With the evolution of sophisticated communication and transportation technologies, the world has become smaller and more interdependent. The global village—once just an abstract idea—is now a reality. Just as technology crosses borders, so do violence and related problems of concern to social workers, such as poverty and unemployment; the use and production of and trafficking in illegal drugs; discrimination; and the oppression of women and children. Increasingly, leaders and citizens are coming to understand that these problems can be solved not by the United States in isolation but by a world community working together. Social workers have a key role to play in this evolving effort.

KEY CONCEPTS

Sustainable Human Development

The term *development* may be defined as "meeting the basic needs of all and extending to all the opportunity to fulfill their aspirations for a better life" (Shuman, 1994, p. 2). According to this broad definition, development focuses on fostering economic opportunity, equity, human rights, dignity, democracy, peace, and spiritual and emotional well-being (Shuman & Harvey, 1993).

Social workers will readily understand this concept, for it is what they strive to do every day

in their work with individuals, families, communities, and organizations. This resource will examine development from a national and international perspective.

Beginning in the late 1980s, a new consensus emerged within the international development community (see page 16) about the best means for achieving long-lasting, positive change in poor countries. The agreed-upon strategy, known as *sustainable human development*, is based on these underlying principles:

- meeting basic human needs for food, clean water, shelter, health care, and education
- expanding economic opportunities for people, especially poor people, to increase their productivity and earning capacity in ways that are environmentally, economically, and socially viable over the long term
- protecting the environment by managing natural resources in ways that take into account the needs of current and future generations
- promoting democratic participation, especially by poor women and men, in economic and political decisions that affect their lives
- encouraging adherence to internationally recognized human rights standards (*At the Crossroads*, 1995).

Global North, Global South

The term *global North* refers to the world's industrialized, wealthy countries, and the term *global South* refers to the world's poor nations. These terms are merely descriptive because the split between rich and poor nations does not fall along strict geographic lines. Social workers in the

The United States spent approximately 1 percent of its annual national budget, or $18 billion, on foreign assistance in 1996. Of this amount, 18 percent, or $3.2 billion, went to fund projects to help people in poor countries better their lives. Other money went toward military and security aid; food, exports, and other economic aid; and operating expenses (*Congressional Quarterly*, 1996).

In addition to federal funds, there are several hundred U.S.-based charitable international development organizations, called private voluntary organizations or nongovernmental organizations. These organizations receive an estimated $4.5 billion a year from individuals and businesses that is used to support relief and development efforts in the poorest nations of the world. Some of the better known organizations are Save the Children, CARE, Oxfam, and the American Red Cross (*Just 1%*, 1995).

United States have traditionally been concerned about poor communities that are hidden in urban centers or in isolated rural areas of this rich nation. Underdeveloped areas of the United States and countries of the global South share many characteristics, such as low standards of living, malnutrition, disease, illiteracy, unemployment, and the lack of adequate medical services.

According to figures on the per capita gross national products of countries throughout the world (World Bank, 1995), there are 24 high-income countries, with 15 percent of the world's people, including the United States, Switzerland, and Japan. Sixty-three countries, containing 29 percent of the world's population, such as the Philippines, Romania, and Iran, make up the middle-income category. And 45 countries, consisting of 56 percent of the world's population, including Guatemala, Somalia, and Bangladesh, constitute the low-income sector.

The global South is where
- about 77 percent of the world's population lives

- almost a billion people live in dire poverty
- about half the people do not know how to read
- a billion people in the labor force are unemployed or underemployed
- typically, the top 20 percent of the population receives 50 percent of the income, and the bottom 20 percent receives less than 5 percent of the income
- 75 percent of rural people do not have access to clean drinking water
- more than half a billion people are hungry and malnourished
- almost 20 percent of the children die before the age of five
- 100 million children are always hungry
- 15 million children die each year from a combination of malnutrition and infection
- the average life expectancy is 54 years compared with 74 years in the global North (Kerschner, 1992; United Nations Children's Fund, 1994).

Violence

Violence may be broadly defined as an act or situation that harms the health or well-being of oneself or others. It includes both direct attacks on a person's physical and psychological integrity and destructive acts that do not involve a direct relationship between victims and the institution or person or persons responsible for the harm (Bulhan, 1985).

One goal of the Violence and Development Project is to expand the common perception of violence to include such problems as racism, sexism, poverty, and hunger. These social ills grow out of institutions, governments, and economic structures that encourage the domination of certain groups of people over other groups and perpetuate unequal access to wealth and other resources. Inequities, which may be based on class, race, gender, or ethnicity, are often enforced by the use of violence by police forces, government troops or their proxies, foreign powers, and other forms of sanctioned militarism.

Threats to personal security and social stability come from several sources (see Table 1). These sources include social and economic systems (deprivation, lack of access, and oppression), the state (repression, torture, and police brutality or inaction), other countries (colonization and war), other groups of people (civil war, ethnic conflict, discrimination, and hate crimes), and individuals or gangs (homicide and muggings). Violence may be directed against specific groups, such as women (rape, domestic violence, and lack of access to higher education or better-paying jobs), children (child abuse and neglect), and ethnic populations (genocide, hate crimes, and discrimination) or against the self (suicide and substance abuse). Among the underlying principles of the Violence and Development Project is that long-term solutions to violence must include permanent changes in structural and institutional systems that give rise to deprivation and oppression and create a world of haves and have-nots.

IN TODAY'S WORLD, INEQUITIES ABOUND

Although more than three-fourths of the world's 5.8 billion people live in the global South, they enjoy only 16 percent of the world's income (UN Development Programme, 1995). One person in four in the global South is unable to satisfy such basic needs as adequate nutrition, safe and sufficient drinking water, clean air to breathe, proper sanitation, and access to health care and elementary education (Sivard, 1993).

Development efforts to address social problems are also needed in the United States. Although this is the richest, most powerful nation in the world, poverty and inequity stubbornly persist. For all its resources, the United States ranks 21st among 132 countries in infant mortality (World Bank, 1995). And despite this country's system of free public education through the secondary level, 50 percent of adults who took part in a nationwide literacy survey scored in the lowest two levels of proficiency, placing them in an at-risk category for low earnings and limited choices for employment (Kirsch, Jungeblut, Jenkins, & Kolstad, 1993). These examples underscore the point that wealth is not necessarily synonymous with greater development.

The common perception is that the global South is fraught with destitution and despair. Yet since 1960, development assistance has helped reduce infant mortality rates in developing countries by 50 percent, increase life expectancy from 46 years to 63 years, and increase primary school enrollment from 48 percent to 78 percent (*Just 1%*, 1995). In some cases, development achievements in poor countries have surpassed those of richer nations. For example, in Honduras, 92 percent of the children under age two are immunized, whereas in Detroit, the rate is 28 percent (Alliance for a Global Community, 1994a). U.S. social workers can learn a great deal from people in the global South who have established

TABLE 1. SOURCES OF THREATS TO PERSONAL SECURITY AND SOCIAL STABILITY

Structural	Institutional	Personal
Avoidable deprivations built into the structure of society based on norms and traditions that subjugate one group in favor of another (poverty, hunger)	Harmful acts by organizations and institutions (oppression, unequal treatment under the law, police brutality, torture)	Interpersonal acts of violence against persons or property (rape, murder, muggings)
	Official forms of violence (state repression, war, and invasion)	Harmful acts against self (alcohol abuse, drug abuse, suicide)
		Acts by organized groups or mobs (hate crimes, looting, rioting)

programs to improve social and economic development in their communities and who understand the need for bettering social institutions as well as individuals.

VIOLENCE AND DEVELOPMENT: MAKING THE CONNECTION

Violence and poverty obstruct the development of human capital—the term used by economists to describe a nation's collective ideas, labor, knowledge, and problem-solving skills. Nations find it difficult or impossible to take care of their own—let alone compete in the international marketplace—when they are burdened with widespread hunger, unemployment, or war. The famine in Somalia that gripped the world's attention in 1992 was the direct result of civil war. The conflict prevented people from planting their crops—food on which they depended to survive.

People continue to fight wars around the world, eating up precious resources that could be used for human development. In 1993, countries in the global South spent as much on military power as the poorest 2 billion people on earth earned in total income (Sivard, 1993). Furthermore, the United States spent $291 billion on military expenditures in 1993—seven times the amount spent by Japan, the country with the next largest military budget (*U.S. Military Spending*, 1993)—and U.S. spending is still on the rise (Hartung, 1994). Thus, in both poor and wealthy countries, military spending drains resources from social programs, widening the disparities between the rich and the poor (Iatridis, 1988; Korotkin, 1985; Sivard, 1993).

REDUCING VIOLENCE THROUGH SUSTAINABLE HUMAN DEVELOPMENT

Examples of successful development projects abound, demonstrating that progress can be made when there is a commitment to developing human potential and the leadership to carry out that commitment. Some projects have been initiated by governments that are serious about alleviating social problems; others have been

spearheaded by a single individual with a driving vision.

The Grameen Bank, founded by economics professor Muhammad Yunus in Bangladesh in 1976, is an example of a cost-effective development initiative that has changed the world. From 1976 to 1994, the bank lent over $1 billion to 2 million people and, in the process, created jobs and supported small businesses (Alliance for a Global Community, 1994b). Nearly half the borrowers have lifted themselves out of poverty.

So successful was Yunus's vision for the poor that his concept of "microenterprise" has been emulated by governments, community groups, and private organizations in Central and South America, Asia, Africa, and the United States. By making small loans (usually less than $100), community-run lending programs enable poor people to boost their earning power, gain greater independence, and better provide for themselves and their children. And with worldwide repayment rates of over 95 percent, such programs have proved that, with support, people can indeed overcome poverty (Alliance for a Global Community, 1994b).

IMPLICATIONS FOR SOCIAL WORKERS

The future of the United States is intertwined with the futures of the nations of the global South. Social work support for human and economic development efforts around the world makes sense as part of an overall program for addressing domestic concerns. Here are a few examples:

1. Global disparities in wealth contribute to political instability and wars, resulting in an influx of refugees and immigrants into the United States. Other nations' wars also affect the United States by limiting the economic growth of its trade partners, by threatening the security of the country's borders and those of its allies, and by causing environmental degradation that crosses national boundaries.

2. Poverty tempts farmers in the global South to engage in the production of illegal drugs, while social workers combat the effects of drug use in this country.

3. Poverty and hunger give poor workers in the global South no choice but to accept jobs with extremely low wages and poor working conditions, with the result that U.S. companies move many of their operations to these countries to take advantage of cheap labor and jobs flow out of the United States. Meanwhile, social workers in this country struggle with the effects of unemployment and increased prejudice and discrimination against immigrants and racial and ethnic groups that is born out of a desire to blame someone for the country's diminishing real incomes.

Social work's ethic of care requires that there be no distinction between "our" poor and "their" poor. The social justice tradition of the profession provides a moral justification for working toward a time when all people will share the world's wealth. Giving poor people access to resources aimed at improving their health, education, and economic status enhances their capability to lead more fulfilling lives and to improve the lot of their children, both of which have lasting implications for the future.

U.S. social workers are uniquely positioned to participate in the international effort to promote global security and development because they have the following capabilities:

- They know how to develop and implement successful interventions to alleviate social problems. In addition, they are trained to consider a problem at the individual, family, community, organizational, and national levels, and the future points toward the inclusion of an international perspective as well.
- They understand the connection between a client's well-being and the political, social, and economic context within which the client lives.
- They adhere to principles that mirror those of successful development, including addressing the basic unmet needs of people first, listening to people and helping them define their own needs, empowering people to make their own decisions, promoting leadership skills, and encouraging democratic participation.

- They have expertise in issues of inner-city development—issues that will be more and more essential as the global South becomes increasingly urbanized.

WHAT YOU CAN DO

Here are some ways in which you can help address problems related to violence and development:

- Learn more about nations of the global South and this country's relationship to them, using the references and resources presented at the end of Part 1 as a start. Talk to people from the countries of the global South who are in the United States. Join a study or travel group.
- Educate yourself about U.S. foreign aid by reading a variety of sources. Support foreign assistance aimed at sustainable human development.
- Learn about, support, and participate in international events, such as the World Summit for Social Development and the World Summit on Children.
- Join organizations that are committed to gun control and reducing violence with the use of guns.
- Learn conflict-resolution strategies as an alternative to violence.
- Teach your children and your young clients respect for people from other countries and cultures. Explain that physical aggression is not the smart way to solve problems and educate them about the consequences of violence.

REFERENCES

Alliance for a Global Community. (1994a). How they compare: Immunization in the U.S. and the developing world. *Connections, 1*(3).

Alliance for a Global Community. (1994b). Micro-enterprise: Small loans, big returns. *Connections, 1*(2).

At the crossroads: The future of foreign aid (Occasional Paper No. 4). (1995). (Available from Bread for the World Institute, 1100 Wayne Avenue, Suite 1000, Silver Spring, MD 20910; phone 301-608-2400)

Bulhan, H. A. (1985). *Frantz Fanon and the psychology of oppression*. New York: Plenum Press.

Congressional Quarterly. (1996, June 1). Weekly report.

Hartung, W. D. (1994). *And weapons for all*. New York: HarperCollins.

Iatridis, D. S. (1988). New social deficit: Neoconservatism's policy of social underdevelopment. *Social Work, 33*, 11–15.

Just 1% (1995). (Brochure available from InterAction, 1717 Massachusetts Avenue, NW, Suite 801, Washington, DC 20036; phone 202-667-8227)

Kerschner, H. K. (1992). *An organizing guide for community-based education and international action*. Washington, DC: American Association for International Aging.

Kirsch, I. S., Jungeblut, A., Jenkins, L., & Kolstad, A. (1993). *Adult literacy in America*. Washington, DC: National Center for Education Statistics.

Korotkin, A. (1985). Impact of military spending on the nation's quality of life. *Social Work, 30*, 369–372.

Shuman, M. (1994). *Toward a global village: International community development initiatives*. Boulder, CO: Pluto Press.

Shuman, M., & Harvey, H. (1993). *Security without war: A post–cold war foreign policy*. Boulder, CO: Westview Press.

Sivard, R. L. (1993). *World military and social expenditures 1993*. Washington, DC: World Priorities.

United Nations Children's Fund. (1994). *The state of the world's children, 1994*. New York: Oxford University Press.

United Nations Development Programme. (1995). *Human development report, 1995*. New York: Oxford University Press.

U.S. military spending: In a league of its own. (1993). (Available from Campaign for New Priorities, 424 C Street, NE, Washington, DC 20002; phone 202-544-8226)

World Bank. (1995). *World Development Report 1995*. New York: Oxford University Press.

ADDITIONAL RESOURCES

Organizations

Alliance for a Global Community
1717 Massachusetts Avenue, NW, Suite 801
Washington, DC 20036
Phone: 202-667-8227
An organization that publishes *Connections*, a newsletter, 10 times a year, with information about the connections between the United States and developing countries.

Brookings Institute
1775 Massachusetts Avenue, NW
Washington, DC 20036
Phone: 202-797-6105
An organization that is engaged in research, education, and publications on important issues of foreign and domestic policy. Publishes the quarterly *Brookings Review*, as well as a variety of books.

Global Exchange
2017 Mission Street, Suite 303
San Francisco, CA 94110
Phone: 415-255-7296 or 1-800-497-1994
An organization that sponsors reality tours and study seminars to Africa, Asia, Latin America, and the Caribbean and publishes books on international issues.

InterAction: American Council for Voluntary International Action
1717 Massachusetts Avenue, NW, Suite 801
Washington, DC 20036
Phone: 202-667-8227
An umbrella organization for several hundred international development agencies with programs throughout the world.

International Activities Committee
Office of Peace and International Affairs
National Association of Social Workers
750 First Street, NE, Suite 700
Washington, DC 20002-4241
Phone: 202-336-8388
or 1-800-638-8799

An NASW committee that oversees and coordinates educational and other programs related to international issues and social work and disseminates a newsletter to NASW members who ask to be placed on the international network.

United Nations Department of Public Information
United Nations, Room S-1040
New York, NY 10017
Phone: 212-963-4475

The department publishes a series of issue papers on topics related to world development, such as the family, human rights, and women, from various UN conferences, for example, the United Nations World Summit for Social Development held in March 1995.

Reports

Human Development Report. Produced by the UN Development Programme (phone 1-800-253-9646) and published annually by Oxford University Press.

Hunger 1995: The Causes of Hunger. Published by Bread for the World Institute (1100 Wayne Avenue, Suite 1000, Silver Spring, MD 20910; phone 301-608-2400).

The State of the World's Children. Produced by the UN Children's Fund and published annually by Oxford University Press. Available at bookstores or from the U.S. Committee for UNICEF (phone 212-686-5522).

World Development Report. Produced by the World Bank and published annually by Oxford University Press (available from the World Bank Bookstore: phone 202-473-2941).

World Military and Social Expenditures. By Ruth Sivard. Published periodically (every three or so years) by and available from World Priorities (phone 202-965-1661).

PART 2

POVERTY

ENSURING ENOUGH FOR
EVERYONE

CHAPTER 2-1

POVERTY

CURRICULUM

Part 2 focuses on poverty as a form of violence and examines connections between poverty and other forms of violence, as well as their links with international development. Some initiatives that were designed to break the poverty trap in other countries are presented as case studies.

GENERAL OBJECTIVES

1. Students will be able to describe parallel conditions of violence in the United States and in less economically advantaged nations.
2. Students will demonstrate a broadened understanding of violence and the role of the social work profession in solving the problem on a global scale.
3. Students will demonstrate an increased interest in learning from successful interventions undertaken by human services workers in the global South and in the United States.
4. Students will be able to define key concepts, such as sustainable human development, global North, and global South.
5. Students will demonstrate an awareness of social work's commitment to social justice by describing how violence and oppression affect vulnerable populations throughout the world.

The objectives and discussion questions in the following section may be used for classroom discussion or in written assignments. They are based on information presented in part 2 of *An Educational Resource* (pp. 35–45 in this volume and pp. 9–19 in the student version).

HUMAN BEHAVIOR IN THE SOCIAL ENVIRONMENT

Objectives

1. Students will demonstrate an understanding of the impact of poverty on the development of individuals and families throughout the life cycle and on the development of communities.
2. Students will be able to explain the multiple causes and effects of poverty, particularly those related to development.

Discussion Questions

1. What are some of the effects of poverty on development across the life span?
2. How are violence and poverty linked at various stages of human development?
3. What are some of the ways in which poverty in the global South is related to poverty in an individual's immediate environment?

SOCIAL WORK THEORY AND PRACTICE

Objectives

1. Students will demonstrate an understanding of the connection between violence in their clients' lives and the political, social, and economic context within which their clients live.
2. Students will be able to articulate practice interventions that are related to sustainable human development and to describe strategies used in the global South that can be adapted for use in the United States.

Discussion Questions

1. Part 2 of *An Educational Resource* (see p. 36 in this text and p. 10 in the student version) lists several causes of poverty. What are the implications of those factors for social work practice interventions?
2. What are the implications of a definition of poverty as a form of passive violence for social work interventions?
3. Case study 2 in *An Educational Resource* (part 2; p. 38 in this text and p. 12 in the student version) describes the struggles of two families with conditions of poverty in Mis-souri and in Mexico. How are these two families connected, both directly and indirectly?

SOCIAL WELFARE POLICY

Objectives

1. Students will demonstrate an understanding of the significance of foreign policy for U.S. social welfare policy.
2. Students will be able to describe specific development projects that have been success-ful in alleviating poverty and violence in the global South and have been replicated in underdeveloped areas in the United States.

Discussion Questions

1. What are the implications for social welfare policy of the gap between rich and poor peo-ple in the United States? What are the impli-cations of the gap between the rich United States and poor countries in the global South?
2. Domestic social welfare policy is concerned with poverty and inequity in the United States. Should social workers in the United States also be concerned with inequities between the global North and the global South? Why or why not?

RESEARCH

Objectives

1. Students will learn to read figures and tables related to poverty, violence, and development.

2. Students will be able to analyze and compare indicators of poverty and social welfare among different countries.

Discussion Questions

1. *An Educational Resource* (p. 37 in this text and p. 11 in the student version) points to a correlation between violent crime and pover-ty. What research evidence is there, if any, to support that contention?
2. On the basis of some of the references listed in part 2 of *An Educational Resource* (for example, *World Military and Social Expenditures* by Ruth Leger Sivard, *Human Development Report* by the United Nations Development Programme, and *Hunger 1995: The Causes of Hunger* by Bread for the World on pp. 44–45 in this text and pp. 18–19 in the student version), what are the indicators of and statistics on social welfare and poverty for several countries in the global South and in the United States? Are they similar or dif-ferent?

FIELD PRACTICUM

Objectives

1. Students will demonstrate an awareness of social work's commitment to social justice by describing how violence and poverty affect vulnerable populations in their field place-ment settings and worldwide.
2. Students will be able to describe specific development projects that have been success-ful in alleviating poverty in the global South and have been replicated in underdeveloped areas of the United States.

Discussion Questions

1. How does poverty affect clients in your field placement? What connections do you see between the conditions of poverty in which your clients live and other forms of vio-lence?
2. Is it possible to be an effective practitioner with poor clients without engaging in commu-nity development strategies? Why or why not?

CASE STUDIES

A Bank for the Poor

Ask the students to read case study 4 about the Grameen Bank in part 2 of *An Educational Resource* (p. 40 in this text and p. 14 in the student version).

Discussion Questions

1. What strengths do poor people bring to the credit scheme described in this case study?
2. How does the Grameen Bank differ from traditional banks?
3. Why do you think the Grameen Bank has been so successful?
4. Hundreds of microenterprise programs have sprung up around the world, including in the United States. Do you think that such a program would work in your community? Why or why not? What modifications would need to be made?

What One Can Learn from India

Ask the students to read case study 5 on the Self-Employed Women's Association (SEWA) in part 2 of *An Educational Resource* (pp. 40–41 in this text and pp. 14–15 in the student version).

Discussion Questions

1. What strengths are apparent in SEWA's approach and in the women who participate in it?
2. What can one learn from SEWA's experience that may be useful in the United States?
3. What role can social workers play in approaches such as this?

Exercise 1—Experiential Classroom Exercise
How Does the World Eat?

Purpose

To help students develop an appreciation of the widespread existence of hunger in the world and an understanding of the inequality of resource distribution and its causes.

Description of Exercise

Divide students into sections simulating division in the world's population and serve them portions of food (such as crackers, slices of fruit, peanuts, popcorn, and bread) that are proportionate to the control of the world's resources.

Learning Activity

1. Obtain the food and divide it up into portions that are equivalent to the distribution of resources throughout the world. Start with a more-than-generous portion for each person. Plan to divide the food so that roughly one-quarter of the students receive either some crumbs or nothing, one-quarter receive a small portion, one-quarter receive a moderate portion, and one-quarter receive a large portion. The last group may be subdivided so that one or two students have even larger portions than the others. For example, for a group of 25 students, start with 25 medium-to-large apples cut into quarters (a total of 100 slices) and apportion the slices as follows:
   - six students: nothing or crumbs
   - seven students: 1 slice each
   - six students: 3 slices each
   - five students: 10 slices each
   - one student: 25 slices.
2. Explain to the class that you are going to serve a simulation snack that reflects how much people around the world get to eat.
3. Randomly assign the students to one of the world's populations by, for example, having them draw a number from a hat to determine their place, and distribute the snack accordingly. Make sure that students who receive large portions are close to those who receive small portions and to those who receive nothing.
4. Ask the students not to eat until they are told to do so.
5. Explain how the distribution corresponds to that in the world. In some countries, such as the United States, there are a few very rich persons, many middle-income persons, and a small number of poor persons who often go hungry. In some countries, such as Sweden, almost everyone has a middle-level income

and no one goes hungry. In some countries, such as India, most of the people are poor and often go hungry, but there are a few rich people and a few middle-income people. In some countries, like China, almost all the people have low to middle incomes. Give the students time to react to the situation.

6. Allow the students to eat. Then explain that the world produces enough food to feed every child, woman, and man the equivalent in calories to what the average person in the United States eats every day.

7. End the exercise by asking the students to take two to three minutes to do some "free writing" about how the exercise affected them, followed by a class discussion.

Discussion

1. Discuss the process—how it related to the real world and relationships among countries, how the students with the biggest portions felt, how the students with the smallest portions felt, how the real world may be able to equalize the availability of food, how the real distribution of food in the world compares to students' previous ideas.

2. Note that inequalities in the distribution of food exist in the United States as well as in other places in the world. Discuss the possible causes of hunger and the possible solutions. Point out that poverty and hunger are a form of violence and discuss the connections between the violence of poverty and the violence of war.

3. Ask the students for their ideas about the distribution of food in the world: how many people go hungry and where they live. Invite them to try to change the distribution of food so it is more equitable. Let them try to design a fair method in their own way. This should be a difficult task. The purpose of this exercise is to give the students a feel for how hard it is for nations of the world to negotiate fair solutions to problems.

Source: Van Soest, 1992, pp. 105–106.

Exercise 2—Discussion of the Myths about Hunger

Purpose

To explore some of the causes of hunger and dispel common myths.

Activity

Have the students read "Myths about Hunger" (pp. 41–42 of *An Educational Resource* in this volume and pp. 15–16 of the student version), followed by a class discussion. This exercise could be used in conjunction with the previous exercise on how the world eats.

Exercise 3—Writing Assignment
Learning about Links between the United States and a Country in the Global South

Purpose

To become familiar with a country in the global South and to gain tools and knowledge to analyze the connections between that country and the United States and the implications of these connections for social work.

Activity

1. Have each student choose a country (other than his or her country of origin) that is considered to be part of the global South, preferably one with which the student has some connection (for example, a client from El Salvador, a field placement in a migrant Guatemalan community, or residence in a state that borders Mexico).

2. Have each student write a two-part paper. The first part (no more than five pages) should be a country profile to familiarize the student with the country he or she selected. It should include the following information:

   a. economic and social conditions and economic performance, with as much data as possible on social and economic

indicators (for example, infant mortality rates, education, health, poverty)
b. recent history and political situation, including relevant current events, and U.S. involvement in the situation, when applicable.

The second part (also no more than five pages) should cover at least two issues or problems that are of major concern to the particular country. Some suggested issues are
- women and development
- illiteracy
- hunger, famine, malnutrition
- debt
- inequality of income and wealth
- unemployment, underemployment, disguised employment
- overpopulation
- war or civil unrest
- children
- environment and development
- violence.

The discussion of each problem should include
a. its nature
b. the human, economic, and social ramifications
c. the probable impact on the United States and other countries in the global North
d. implications of that impact for the social work profession, the student's practice and clients, and social welfare policy.

Exercise 4—Short Lecture and Quiz on Dispelling Myths

Purpose

To help social workers understand the reality of the interdependence of the United States and the global South.

Introduction: Lecture

Important lessons can be learned from sustainable development approaches around the world that are aimed at addressing poverty and related problems. Unfortunately, social workers usually view unemployment, crime, and poverty in the United States as separate from problems in the global South, so they do not learn those lessons. Yet, the threat that global poverty will affect the lives of all people—in rich and in poor nations—is real and persistent, and there are no global safeguards against the related threats of crime and drug wars in the streets. Thus, it is imperative for social workers to recognize the interdependence of poverty and violence in the United States and in the global South. However, there are several barriers to learning from colleagues in the global South:

Lack of information. North Americans in general have an incomplete and inaccurate image of countries in the global South. They have little knowledge of poor countries, and reports in newspapers and on television of exceptional events, such as famines and floods, foster misperceptions. Although most people know about the famines, wars, and corruption that plague such countries as Rwanda, Haiti, and Somalia, few know about the many successful programs for development, relief, and refugees.

Sense of hopelessness. Social workers tend to share the general public's widespread impression that countries of the global South are dominated by poverty, violence, and human misery. Thus, they overestimate the needs of people in the global South and feel overwhelmed, hopeless, and helpless in the face of what they perceive to be enormous problems. There is a sense that the global South is simply too far gone for social work efforts to make any real impact.

Self-interest. People in this country tend to think that foreign assistance is a drain on the U.S. economy and has no benefits for them or this country's problems. Many North Americans continue to believe that the world is divided into domestic and foreign—the First and Third Worlds, the North and the South, us and them.

Focus on short-term crises. Pressing foreign policy concerns—often connected with war, conflict, and violence—receive most of the attention of Congress and the bulk of the money for foreign assistance and take attention away from sustainable development. Similarly, domestic crises (often related to crime and violence) take attention away from sustainable development in the United States.

Activity

The section on Myths about Poverty and International Development in part 2 of *An Educational Resource* (see pp. 42–44 of this volume and pp. 16–18 of the student version) can be used to stimulate classroom discussion aimed at helping social work students overcome blocks to learning about poverty and violence in an international context. In addition, the following short quiz can be administered before the discussion.

1. What percentage of the world's children do you think are starving, defined as visibly malnourished?

2. What percentage of the world's families are living in absolute poverty so they cannot meet even their most basic needs?

3. What percentage of the world's children, age 6 to 12 start school?

4. Is the rate of population growth in the global South increasing, decreasing, or staying about the same?

5. What percentage of the income of the countries of the global South comes from overseas aid?

6. Are loan repayments from countries in the global South more or less than the aid they receive?

7. Where does most of the disaster relief to the global South come from?

8. What percentage of U.S. trade do you think is with the global South?

9. What percentage of the world's population do you think live in the global South?

10. What percentage of the U.S. federal budget do you think is spent on foreign assistance?

11. Is the United States the most generous foreign assistance donor in the world?

12. Do you think most U.S. foreign aid dollars are spent in the United States or in the global South?

13. What percentage of the world's population do you think live in North America?

1. 1 percent to 2 percent.

2. 20 percent to 25 percent.

3. 90 percent.

4. It is decreasing in every region of the global South, including Africa.

5. Aid amounts to about 1 percent of the incomes of the countries of the global South.

6. Loan repayments from poor countries exceed the aid the countries receive.

7. Most disaster relief comes from within the global South through efforts by indigenous people and organizations or from other poor countries.

8. In the 1980s, two-fifths of U.S. exports were purchased by countries in the global South, and 10 of the 20 U.S. trade partners were in the global South. The debt crisis and drought that the global South has experienced since then may have slowed the rate at which poor countries import U.S. goods. Nevertheless, from 1985 to 1995, exports to the global South rose from $71 billion to $180 billion.

9. In 1980, 74 percent of the world's 4.5 billion people lived in the global South. By 2000, when the world's population is expected to reach 6.1 billion, 79 percent will live in the global South.

10. U.S. foreign aid expenditures are currently less than 1 percent of federal outlays, compared with 15 percent during the Marshall Plan in the late 1940s.

11. No. The United States is now fourth behind Japan, France, and Germany as the largest donor of official development assistance—in dollars. However, as a percentage of the GNP con tributed, the United States is 21st behind Norway, Denmark, Sweden, Netherlands, France, Canada, Luxembourg, Switzerland, Australia, Portugal, Germany, Austria, Belgium, Finland, the United Kingdom, Japan, Spain, Italy, Ireland, and New Zealand.

12. More than half the U.S. foreign aid dollars are spent in the United States on goods and services provided to the global South.

13. 6 percent.

REFERENCE

Van Soest, D. (1992). *Incorporating peace and social justice into the social work curriculum*. Washington, DC: National Association of Social Workers, Office of Peace and International Affairs.

FOR FURTHER READING

Collins, S. D., Ginsburg, H. L., & Schaffner Goldberg, G. (1994). *Jobs for all: A plan for the revitalization of America*. New York: Apex Press.

According to these authors, the defining characteristics of the New World Order appear to be chronic unemployment, underemployment, and declining wages. They analyze the impact of domestic and global economic restructuring on American workers, families, and communities and propose a comprehensive program of Jobs for All as a solution to many of the social, economic, and environmental problems plaguing American society. Although the proposed program focuses primarily on domestic policy, it takes account of the need for an extension of its principles to the international arena. Toward this end, the authors propose a global "New Deal" program to improve the living standards of the world's poor majority, within a framework that provides for the rights of workers, human rights, and environmental protection.

Danaher, K. (Ed.). (1994). *50 years is enough: The case against the World Bank and the International Monetary Fund*. Boston: South End Press.

This book contains excellent critiques by 36 authors of the global economic context, country case studies, women, the environment, tribal people, internal scandals, and alternatives. It includes resources and a guide to organizations.

De Silva, D. (Project Coordinator). (1989). *Against all odds: Breaking the poverty trap*. Washington, DC: Panos Institute.

This book describes how ordinary people have broken through the poverty trap in India, Tanzania, Bangladesh, Kenya, Sri Lanka, Indonesia, and Zambia. Journalists from each country visited sites of development projects and listened to the people whom the projects are intended to benefit. This interesting book is a compilation of their reports.

Epstein, G., Graham, J., & Nemhard, J. (1993). *Creating a new world economy: Force of change and plans for action*. Philadelphia: Temple University Press.

This book, written by economists, analyzes the emerging global economy on the basis of the authors' research and experience teaching economics to activists from community movements; labor unions; and environmental, feminist, and other groups. It is designed for those who think that the purpose of gaining knowledge is to change the world for the better.

CHAPTER 2-2

POVERTY

EDUCATIONAL RESOURCE

Everyone has the right to a standard of living adequate for the health and well-being of himself and his family, including food, clothing, housing and medical care, and necessary social services.

—*Universal Declaration of Human Rights,* Article 25

Poverty anywhere is a threat to prosperity everywhere.

—*Human Development Report, 1993*

Over the past 50 years, many gains have been made in raising the standard of living for people around the globe. Nevertheless, poverty remains ubiquitous:

- One-fifth of all human beings live in absolute poverty, without adequate food, clothing, and shelter (United Nations [UN], 1995c).
- Fifteen percent of people in the United States—one of the most affluent countries in the world—live below the poverty line (UN Development Programme, 1994).
- In the global South, about 1.3 billion people (almost one-third of the population) live below the poverty line. Nearly 800 million people do not get enough food (UN Development Programme, 1995).

In spite of efforts to close the gap between the rich and the poor, inequities persist. Between 1960 and 1991, the share of the world's income for the richest 20 percent of the global population increased from 70 percent to 85 percent. During the same period, the already meager share of the world's income for the poorest 20 percent of the global population decreased from 2.3 percent to 1.4 percent (UN Development Programme, 1994). Discrepancies between the wealth of the global North and the global South are equally striking. Wealthy nations in general have almost tripled their per capita incomes since 1950. In contrast, the per capita incomes in the poorest countries—home to 77 percent of the world's population—have stagnated (Epstein, Graham, & Nemhard, 1993).

Poverty and inequity are passive forms of violence that impede human development (New York City NASW chapter Center, 1994). Mahatma Gandhi characterized poverty as the worst form of violence (Dasgupta, 1968). Part 2 examines the conditions and consequences of poverty, both at home and abroad. It discusses the connections between poverty, violence, and development and considers some initiatives that have been designed to break the poverty trap.

POVERTY DEFINED

Absolute poverty refers to the inability to obtain the goods and services needed to meet socially defined minimum needs. In the United States, the official government measure of absolute poverty is based on the minimum annual amount of money required to sustain a family ($14,335 for a family of four in 1992) (DiNitto, 1995, p. 69).

According to the definition of *relative poverty*, a person is poor when his or her income is significantly less than the average income of the general population. This definition focuses on inequality of incomes, rather than the absence of resources to provide for absolute needs (Schiller, 1989).

WHAT CAUSES POVERTY?

Despite the historic tendency to blame poor people for their problems, the vast majority of people do not choose to be poor. Rather, throughout the world, poverty is a result of many factors, among them:

- lack of access to economic "building blocks," such as land, seeds, water, tools, training, and education
- unemployment or underemployment
- inequitable distribution of global resources, including food
- inadequate government support for needed social supports
- discrimination against ethnic and racial groups and women, who are disproportionately represented among poor people
- war and military spending, which drain limited resources that could be used for human development.

There are considerable differences between the poverty conditions faced by people in the industrialized global North and the mass poverty experienced by people in the global South. But poor people worldwide have one thing in common: They do not receive sufficient support. Many people have an inflated idea of how much help the U.S. government is giving poor people. This perception was reflected in a 1995 survey of 1,200 U.S. voters, 19 percent of whom cited welfare as the biggest item in the federal budget and 27 percent of whom cited foreign aid. In reality, welfare was only 1.1 percent of the federal budget in 1995, and foreign aid was even less than that (*U.S. Budget for FY '97*, 1996).

POVERTY, VIOLENCE, AND DEVELOPMENT: MAKING CONNECTIONS

Poverty is violence—violence against people. Physical, mental, psychological, intellectual, emotional, social, legal, political, you-name-it violence. It is ugly and angry and everywhere.

—Lourie, 1968, p. 1

Poverty Affects Human Health

Worldwide, threats to health are typically greater for the poorest people, particularly children in rural areas. In the global South, an estimated 17 million people die from infectious and parasitic diseases each year. Most of these deaths are linked with poor nutrition and unsafe living conditions, including polluted water (UN Development Programme, 1994).

Statistics on health care are also bleak. There is but one physician for every 7,000 people in the global South versus one physician for every 400 people in the more prosperous global North. Yet, even though people in the global North are more likely to have access to health care than are people elsewhere, 40 million low-income Americans still did not have health insurance in 1996—up from 35 million in 1989 and 37 million in 1993 (UN Development Programme, 1994; Wines & Pear, 1996).

Poverty Impedes Child Development

According to the UN (1995a), in the global South,
- about 13 million children under age five die each year from easily preventable diseases and malnutrition
- an estimated 130 million children, almost two-thirds of them girls, lack access to primary education
- an estimated 200 million youngsters are forced to work for their own or their families' survival, often under dangerous and exploitative conditions.

Poverty takes its toll on children in the United States as well:

Across an astonishing range of outcomes—including premature death, stunted growth, physical impairment, injury, learning disability, low educational achievement, school failure, abuse and neglect, extreme behavioral problems, and delinquency—poor children fare worse than children who grow up in families that are able to meet their basic needs. (Sherman, 1994, p. 16)

Poverty Breeds Shame, Fear, and Anger

Economic hardship contributes to parental stress and depression. Case study 1, of Anne and Susan, is one mother's account of the horrible effects of poverty on her and her daughter.

CASE STUDY 1
Anne and Susan

Susan was raised in poverty and I am still learning the many ways it hurt her. I [Anne] am her mother. Susan was born two weeks after my 18th birthday and by the time she was 12, we had moved more than 30 times, always one step ahead of or behind the eviction notices, gas and light disconnect notices, and various other bills haunting our mailbox. We laughed a lot and tried to make it an adventure, like the time she was six and the two of us had to move our bed across town on a bus.

But then I would cry and cry for days at a time. Being poor made me crazy, and Susan learned to be my support, caretaker, and defender before she could read.

A few times I tried to kill myself out of fear and shame at not being able to keep a roof over our heads, out of anger over not being able to keep a job and needing to return over and over again to welfare, out of desperation whenever the welfare department would cut off my eligibility by mistake.

Poverty was more than not having enough. It was about not having any control over the most intimate parts of our lives, and, for me, about feeling shame, fear, and anger all the time. After more than 20 low-wage jobs, I enrolled in college when Susan was eight. A few years later, we received a rent subsidy which allowed us to stay in one place. Things got a bit better. For the first time in either of our lives, we had [a] community, permanent friends, and a sense of belonging. Today, Susan and I are successful professionals, and best friends. It didn't take much: a rent subsidy, a generous state university admissions policy, and access to mental health services. The rest we did on our own (From *Wasting America's Future* by Arloe Sherman, ©1994 by Children's Defense Fund, reprinted by permission of Beacon Press, Boston, p. 30).

Poverty Contributes to Violence

Juvenile crime and violence are highly correlated with poverty and other factors related to underdevelopment, including unemployment and inadequate education and social services (UN Development Programme, 1994). The same holds true for adult crime and violence. "Despite some findings to the contrary, a significant correlation has been shown to exist among societal inequality, discrimination, and homicide. Among all groups in the U.S., regardless of race, homicide is found disproportionately among the lowest socioeconomic groups" (Hawkins, 1990, p. 160). In Washington, DC, for example, the poorest part of the city has a violent crime rate 13 times higher than the wealthiest part (Sherman, 1994).

Poverty and inequity set the stage for ethnic conflict as well. Contrary to widespread belief, violence does not spring naturally from ethnic differences:

Modern states . . . create an economic barrier between mainstream populations—the rich and the educated—and ethnic populations—the poor and the marginalized. The ensuing power struggles generate the sorts of violent civil conflict that many observers attribute to some sort of natural hostility. But [different ethnic groups] are not predetermined enemies, and when these peoples have adequate space and autonomy, their basic capacity for respect and problem-solving will flourish. (Boulding, 1995, p. 9)

Inadequate and Ineffective Development Contribute to Poverty

In the 1950s and 1960s, several nations in the global South implemented ambitious development programs using Western technology and aid. Because of poor planning, many of these programs served only to marginalize struggling people further. When mechanized farm technology, designed to increase crop yields, was introduced in Iran, for example, scores of laborers were no longer needed. These laborers were forced to migrate to overcrowded cities, where they found little work or other services (Rohr, 1989).

In poor countries, industrial initiatives that are motivated solely by the desire for profits and that confer value on individuals only to the extent that they produce profits merely exploit the very people who should benefit from them (UN Development Programme, 1994). Case study 2, of Randy Conway and Angelica Hernandez, highlights the negative effects of unjust development on two families, one in the United States, the other in the global South.

CASE STUDY 2
Randy Conway and Angelica Hernandez

Randy Conway is 44 years old and lives with his wife and three children in the small town of Mount Vernon, Missouri. He worked 20 years in a Zenith factory making televisions. Zenith had moved from the northern United States to Missouri in 1976, in search of workers who were willing to toil for lower wages and without the benefit of trade unions. By 1992, Randy was making $11 per hour, but then Zenith moved 20,000 of its U.S. jobs to Mexico, including most of the jobs in Missouri. Randy is now out of work. Zenith spokesman John Taylor admitted that "the wage structure in Mexico is a primary reason for our relocation there."

Angelica Hernandez has worked in Zenith's Reynosa, Mexico, factory since 1988. She works in a noisy plant with hazardous chemicals all around and takes home $35 for a 48-hour week. Angelica, her husband, and their seven children live in a dirt-floor shack, 12 feet by 18 feet, that has no electricity and no running water (GATT and NAFTA, n.d.).

Summarizing the North–South Poverty Link

The global North and the global South are linked in several ways:

1. Keeping wages suppressed in the global South causes companies to relocate jobs from high-wage countries like the United States to developing countries. The result: unemployment at home and exploitation of workers in the global South.

2. Poverty in the global South forces people to migrate to prosperous countries in search of jobs and other opportunities. Immigrants often face racism and ethnic violence in their adopted countries, particularly when they settle in financially stretched communities. Many families are separated in the process of migrating. Consequently, newcomers are further isolated.

3. Countries that are desperate to pay off their debts pillage their natural resources to gain new income, and their actions promote global warming and water pollution (Danaher, 1994).

ALLEVIATING POVERTY THROUGH SUSTAINABLE HUMAN DEVELOPMENT

Three interrelated strategies—reducing poverty, creating employment, and increasing social integration—are at the core of sustainable human development. These strategies are consistent with principles embodied in the Universal Declaration of Human Rights (UN, 1985).

The UN Development Programme (1994) recommended that countries pursue the following measures to alleviate poverty:

- provide poor people with access to basic services, such as health care, housing, and clean water

- invest in education, training, and skills development, especially for women
- ensure equal access to land, agricultural resources, credit, and information
- involve poor people in the design of poverty-reduction strategies
- create a market environment that facilitates new employment opportunities
- guarantee basic legal rights to all
- implement antidiscrimination measures and apply stiff penalties for violations
- support grassroots organizations that provide citizens with direct participation in decision making.

Communities Mobilize to Tackle Poverty

Change is occurring in local communities around the world as women's groups, peasant groups, religious organizations, consumer advocates, and environmental protection societies work to break the poverty trap (Breslin, 1995). Case study 3, of Wangari Maathai, describes how the actions of one individual can evolve into a communitywide development initiative that empowers people to reduce poverty.

CASE STUDY 3
Wangari Maathai

In 1977, Wangari Maathai went into her backyard in Kenya and planted seven small trees. "I realized that when you talk about the problems, you tend to make people feel that there is nothing they can do. To break that cycle, one has to start with a positive step. Planting a tree is very simple—something positive that anybody can do."

As a member of the National Council of Women of Kenya, Maathai enlisted some women farmers to plant more trees. In the beginning, Mobil Oil Corporation provided funding for tree nurseries. Now the funding comes from nonprofit organizations and in the form of small donations from women all over the world. The nurseries that supply the indigenous trees are located in rural areas where they provide jobs for local people who then train other local people how to grow and plant them.

People not only get the benefit of the trees and earn a living but take responsibility for their environment and themselves. The Green Belt movement has also grown to include training for women in nutrition and family planning and has expanded its agenda to challenge oppressive social institutions.

As Maathai put it, "The Green Belt Movement is a movement to empower people, to raise their consciousness, to give them hope. It shows them that the power to change their environment is within themselves, and within their own capacities" (Maathai, 1988, p. 1).

Role of Nongovernmental Organizations

Thousands of nongovernmental organizations (NGOs) around the world are playing an important role in addressing poverty and related problems through empowering citizens and engaging in international advocacy for the rights of marginalized people. Vital lessons can be learned from the development approaches of NGOs that encourage communities to take control of their futures (UN, 1995b). In Tanzania, for example, the Community Development Trust Fund helped members of a poor village establish their own health clinic and encouraged residents' participation in all phases of the project (Ngaiza, 1989).

Grassroots Economic Alternatives

A new wave of grassroots organizations in the global South and the United States are redefining economic development to incorporate principles of equity, democratic participation, and environmental sustainability (GATT and NAFTA, n.d.) using two strategies: cooperatives and revolving credit.

- Cooperatives. In countries as diverse as Zimbabwe and Mexico, family farmers have formed cooperatives to produce and market their products. In the mountains of Mexico's Guerrero province, for example, campesinos have organized a regional alliance of cooperatives to manage their coffee and honey exports (GATT and NAFTA, n.d.).
- Revolving credit. Most of the world's poor people suffer from the lack of access to credit.

Many groups have been pooling and lending capital to the poor to enable them to start small businesses or to improve farming practices (*GATT and NAFTA*, n.d.).

Case studies 4 and 5 present examples of how poor people in the global South have improved their lives through grassroots efforts.

CASE STUDY 4
A Bank for Poor People

In 1976, Muhammad Yunus, a professor-turned-banker, offered tiny loans to the poorest people in one village in Bangladesh. The people proved to be good at using the money to earn income and at paying back the loans. Although the poor borrowers were honest and hardworking, conventional bankers did not choose to see them as such and would not give them loans.

Because of the encouraging results of Yunus's initial loan program, the program was expanded to two villages, then to 10 villages, to one district and then to five districts in Bangladesh. Throughout the process, conventional bankers kept saying, "What you are seeing is not the real thing. The real thing is that the poor have no will to work, they have no ability. They will never return your money" (Yunus, 1994, p. xi). However, people continued to pay back the money, and the program kept expanding. As Yunus (1994) noted:

> Today, Grameen Bank, the poor people's bank in Bangladesh, operates in 34,000 villages, exactly half the number of all the villages in Bangladesh. Grameen Bank currently lends money to 1.7 million borrowers, 94% of whom are women. The borrowers own the bank. We lend out over $30 million each month in loans averaging less than $100. The repayment rate for our loans is over 98%. Besides income-generating loans, we also give housing loans. A typical housing loan is $300. We have given more than 220,000 housing loans so far with a perfect repayment record. Studies done on Grameen tell us that the borrowers have improved their income, widened their asset base and moved steadily toward crossing the poverty line and toward a life of dignity and honor. Studies also tell us that in Grameen families the nutrition level is better than in non-Grameen families, child mortality is lower and adoption of family-planning practices is higher. All studies confirm the visible empowerment of women. (p. xi)

The Grameen Bank is different from other banks in many ways. For example, to build commitment and provide community support, a prospective client must find five friends to borrow with. Considerable time is spent preparing the five-member group to learn how to make decisions and to operate as a community. For instance, questions are raised with the group about their reactions if one of them should fail to pay his or her weekly installment. The advice that is repeatedly given to the group is this:

> Please never get angry with the person who cannot pay the installment. Please don't put pressure on her to make her pay. Be a good friend, don't turn into an enemy. As a good friend, your first response should be, "Oh my God, she is in trouble, we must go and help her out." (Yunus, 1994, p. xii)

The Grameen Bank is based on the principle that the borrower knows best, and borrowers are encouraged to make their own decisions within the context of community and responsibility to each other. The money that is paid back by borrowers provides the resources for further loans, and the five-member group develops as a franchise.

CASE STUDY 5
What One Can Learn from India

The Self-Employed Women's Association (SEWA) holds to the simple yet radical belief that poor women need organizing, not welfare. Based in a dusty old textile town called Ahmedabad on the edge of a desert, SEWA is a trade union for self-employed people. It offers union membership to people such as the illiterate women who sell vegetables for 50 cents a day in the city markets or who pick up paper scraps for recycling from the streets.

When a woman joins SEWA, her income increases because the power of the union allows her to obtain better prices from the middlemen who supply her vegetables or who purchase her scraps of paper. Then she puts the extra income toward her family's education and health care or birth control. The oppressed Indian woman also begins to change the way she thinks of herself when she joins SEWA. She starts to see herself as a worker, an active producer—not just someone's wife or daughter-in-law. When her self-image begins to change, she meets women from other communities, and the barriers of caste begin to break down.

SEWA has a membership of 150,000 women, the vast majority of whom are poor and illiterate. It has organized women into 70 different trade cooperatives, from fish vending to cattle raising to weaving to hand rolling small Indian cigarettes. SEWA now provides health care and insurance for its members. In addition, SEWA continues to expand, with its reputation growing well beyond the borders of India.

What does all this mean for the United States? At a time when the United States seems intent on ending welfare as it now exists, SEWA may provide a model. From the dust bowls of India to the South Bronx of New York City, a simple truth has emerged: Give people some control over their destinies and watch as a spirit of enterprise emerges. Another truth that has become apparent around the world is that women are the real agents for change, both in the United States and in the global South.

Credit for All

Study after study on credit schemes for poor people has confirmed that poor people are credit worthy:

- Poor people can save, even if only a little.
- Poor people are reliable borrowers. Repayment rates of 90 percent and more are not rare.
- Poor people are able and willing to pay market interest rates, so that credit schemes for poor people stand a good chance of becoming viable, self-financing undertakings.
- Credit schemes for poor people work because they significantly improve people's incomes— typically by more than 20 percent and, at times, by more than 100 percent (UN Development Programme, 1994).

MYTHS ABOUT HUNGER

Myth: People are hungry because there is not enough food in the world. If poor people stopped having so many children, there would be enough food for everyone.

Reality: Rapid population growth is an important contributor to world hunger. However, the inequitable distribution of resources and the overconsumption of resources by affluent people are equally significant causes. The world produces enough food for everyone to have 2,500 calories a day—150 more than the basic minimum—if food is distributed and consumed equally. Although wealthy people, mostly in industrialized countries, make up only 20 percent of the world's population, they control 85 percent of its income and consume 80 percent of its resources (*Hunger 1995*, 1995).

Myth: Hunger is not a problem in the United States.

Reality: In the United States, an estimated 30 million people cannot afford to buy enough food to maintain good health, and 12 million children under age 18 are hungry. In 1992, the last year for which information is available, 15 percent of U.S. residents—38 million people—lived below the poverty line and faced the threat of hunger (*Hunger 1995*, 1995).

Myth: There is not much of a connection between violence and hunger.

Reality: Hunger and poverty breed violence. People who live in an affluent society but cannot obtain the necessary income to feed, clothe, and house their families sometimes turn to violence, crime, and selling drugs as their only means of survival. In the United States, someone dies from a gunshot wound every 14 minutes. Acutecare hospitals in Washington, DC, spend more than $20 million a year treating injuries from violent crime. Moreover, the incidences of homicide and suicide are higher in low-income communities than in middle-class communities (*Hunger 1995*, 1995). To end the vicious cycle of violence in this country, hunger must be alleviated.

Myth: No one has to be hungry. All people can pull themselves up by their bootstraps.

Reality: Race, ethnicity, gender, and age all have a powerful impact on who is hungry and who eats. Structural-level violence ensures that the system of inequity continues even when people work hard to provide for their basic needs. Worldwide, racial and ethnic minorities and women lack equal access to resources, have fewer opportunities, and thus are less able to provide for themselves and more vulnerable to hunger (*Hunger 1995*, 1995).

MYTHS ABOUT POVERTY AND INTERNATIONAL DEVELOPMENT

Myth: The global South is composed of poor countries that are overwhelmingly dominated by poverty, violence, and human misery. The problems are so enormous that there is really nothing that anyone can do.

Reality: The countries of the global South have average annual per capita gross national products (GNPs) of less than $2,000 and are faced with problems related to poverty, hunger, overpopulation, education, health, environment, and debt (Kerschner, 1991). However, there is a widespread tendency to overestimate the needs of people in the global South and thus to feel hopeless and helpless in the face of what is perceived as enormous problems, as in the list of misperceptions (Kerschner, 1991) in the next column.

Myth: In spite of billions of dollars spent in foreign aid, conditions continue to be just as bad in the global South.

Reality: Conditions have greatly improved for people in the global South since 1950 as a result of four decades of assistance from the United States, other industrialized nations, and poor countries themselves. The record of human development is unprecedented, with the global South setting a pace three times faster than industrial countries did a century ago. Rising rates of life expectancy, falling rates of infant mortality, increasing educational attainment, and much improved nutrition are a few of the heartening indicators.

During the 1980s and continuing into the 1990s, social progress in many African and Latin American countries slowed down and, in some cases, retreated. Yet the immense progress made during the previous three decades illustrates the value of cooperative development. For example, it took only 35 years to lower the infant mortality rate in the global South from 200 per thousand to 70 per thousand live births, an achievement it took European countries a century to gain; be-tween 1950 and 1986, life expectancy increased from 37 to 61 years in low-income countries; by 1986, 60 percent of the population of the global South could read, compared with only 30 percent in 1950 (Kerschner, 1991; UN Development Programme, 1994). According to UNICEF (1994), 24 countries in the global South have already reduced malnutrition by 10 percent or more, and 30 of 61 other poor countries for which information was available were on track to reduce child malnutrition by 20 percent by 1995.

Misperception	Fact
Most of the world's children are starving.	1 percent to 2 percent of the world's children are visibly malnourished.
The vast majority of the world's families are living in absolute poverty.	20 percent to 25 percent of the world's families are poor.
Only 10 percent to 20 percent of the world's six- to 12-year-old children start school.	Almost 90 percent of the world's six- to 12-year-old children start school.
The rate of population growth in the global South is increasing.	The rate of population growth is decreasing in every region of the global South, including Africa.

Myth: The United States is the most generous foreign-assistance provider in the world.

Reality: The United States has dropped to fourth place behind Japan, France, and Germany in the amount it spends on foreign aid (in dollars). However, as a percentage of the GNP contributed, the United States is 21st, with foreign aid expenditures of less than 1 percent of federal outlays, compared to 15 percent during the Marshall Plan in the late 1940s (Kerschner, 1991; Lippmann, 1996).

Myth: Most disaster relief to the global South comes from industrialized nations in the global North.

Reality: Most disaster relief comes from the global South through efforts by indigenous people and organizations or from other poor countries.

Myth: Only a small percentage of U.S. trade is with poor countries.

Reality: Nine out of 10 countries that are leading importers of U.S. commodities, such as South Korea and Thailand, were once recipients of U.S. foreign assistance (Alliance for a Global Community, 1995). From 1985 to 1995, U.S. exports to developing countries more than doubled—from $71 billion to $180 billion. Every additional $1 billion in exported goods resulted in 20,000 new U.S. jobs (*Just 1%*, 1995).

Myth: Foreign assistance only helps other countries, the United States reaps no benefits from it, and it does not alleviate the problems in this country with which social workers are concerned.

Reality: It is important to understand how foreign assistance is linked to social problems in the United States. By helping countries in the global South to deal with and solve their problems, we Americans are inevitably helping ourselves and addressing our own problems. The following examples illustrate how foreign aid is not simply assistance to other countries but a form of social work intervention that addresses problems and assists clients in the United States through global cooperation.

- Foreign assistance can be seen as a social work intervention to combat unemployment and the decrease in the number of jobs in the United States caused by the movement of industries to developing countries. Many of the estimated billion people in the global South who live in absolute poverty are forced to work for little money in dangerous and extremely poor working conditions, which makes them attractive resources for corporate profits. They also have no money to buy U.S. products; in the 1980s, for instance, the United States lost 1.5 million to 2 million jobs because of diminished purchasing power in the developing world. As a result of economic and social development, workers in a more prosperous developing world could demand higher wages and decent working conditions and would have more money to spend on imported U.S. products, thereby creating jobs and reducing this country's trade deficit (Shuman, 1994).

- Foreign assistance can be seen as a preventive measure to address the large number of refugees who enter the United States with multiple problems as a result of having undergone tremendous suffering. Violence, oppression, and poverty in Africa, Asia, the Middle East, and Latin America have driven hundreds of thousands of people from their homelands to this country, presenting a new array of challenges to the U.S. mental health and social services delivery systems. Conditions that lead to the displacement of millions of refugees—wars, oppression, persecution, and poverty—are usually connected with economic and social factors related to underdevelopment. By improving social and economic conditions in the global South, the United States would decrease the need for people to leave their countries involuntarily.

- Because the illegal drug problem in the United States is connected to poverty in the global South, assistance with economic development can be viewed as preventive intervention in dealing with substance abuse. More than 26 million North Americans abuse illegal drugs, and an estimated four-fifths of these narcotics—including almost all the heroin and cocaine—come from other countries (UN Development Programme, 1994). The primary illegal drug–producing countries are in the global South. For example, coca, which is used to make cocaine, is grown by poor Latin American and South American farmers who can make several times the profits selling coca that they could get from other crops. The United States has been blamed for creating an incentive for farmers to divert crops from coffee to coca because of its failure to support the renewal of an international coffee agreement that triggered a 50 percent drop in world coffee prices (Kerschner, 1991). Moreover, the income generated from drug-related crops helps the debt-ridden poor countries repay their foreign loans. Unless people in the global South have hope for other means of survival, they will continue to grow illegal drugs, and the United States will continue to have an enormous drug abuse problem.

WHAT YOU CAN DO

- Focus on the development needs identified by the communities in which you work. Take advantage of existing community structures and skills to combat poverty and exploitation.
- Learn about the outcome of the UN World Summit for Social Development, held in Copenhagen on March 6–12, 1995. Information on the UN Declaration for Social Development and the Program of Action is available from Lilian Chatterjee, ICSW Information, International Council on Social Welfare (380 Saint-Antoine Street West, Suite 3200, Montreal, Quebec, Canada H2Z 3X7; phone 514-287-3280, fax 514-987-1567).
- Learn about the Universal Declaration of Human Rights (UN, 1985). Adopted by the UN in 1948, the declaration was the first statement on the fundamental rights of all human beings. Its provisions have been incorporated into the laws and constitutions of many countries.

- Organize a teach-in on the politics of welfare reform at your college or university. One such event took place at the Graduate School of Social Service, Fordham University, New York City, in June 1994. Its goals: to protest recent welfare reform proposals that blame social problems on poor families, to dispel myths about the current debate on welfare reform, and to call for change.
- Learn about structural adjustment programs and their consequences. A good place to start is to read Danaher's (1994) *50 Years Is Enough*.

REFERENCES

Alliance for a Global Community. (1995). Hunger: Here and there. *Connections, 2*(2).

Boulding, E. (1995, February). The many dimensions of peacebuilding. *Hunger TeachNet, 6*(1), 8–11.

Breslin, P. (1995, April). On these sidewalks of New York, the sun is shining again. *Smithsonian, 26*, 100–111.

Danaher, K. (Ed.). (1994). *50 years is enough: The case against the World Bank and the International Monetary Fund.* Boston: South End Press.

Dasgupta, S. (1968). Gandhian concept of nonviolence and its relevance today to professional social work. *Indian Journal of Social Work, 29*, 113–122.

DiNitto, D. (1995). *Social welfare: Politics and public policy* (4th ed.). Boston: Allyn & Bacon.

Epstein, G., Graham, J., & Nemhard, J. (1993). *Creating a new world economy: Forces of change and plans for action.* Philadelphia: Temple University Press.

GATT and NAFTA: How trade agreements can change your life. (n.d.). (Available from Global Exchange, 2017 Mission Street, Room 303, San Francisco, CA 94110; phone 415-255-7296)

Hawkins, D. (1990). Explaining the black homicide rate. *Journal of Interpersonal Violence, 5*, 151–163.

Hunger 1995: Causes of hunger. (1995).(Available from Bread for the World Institute, 1100 Wayne Avenue, Suite 1000, Silver Spring, MD 20910; phone 301-608-2400)

Just 1%. (1995). (Brochure available from InterAction, 1717 Massachusetts Avenue, NW, Suite 801, Washington, DC 20036; phone 202-667-8227)

Kerschner, H. (1991). *A primer on international development.* Washington, DC: American Association for International Aging.

Lippmann, T. (1996, June 18). U.S. loses rank in global giving. *Washington Post*.

Lourie, N. V. (1968, September 28). *Poverty is violence*. Speech given at a meeting of the Women's Inter-national League for Peace and Freedom, Philadelphia.

Maathai, W. (1988). *The green belt movement*. Nairobi, Kenya: Environment Liaison Center International.

New York City NASW Center on Poverty, Violence, and Development. (1994). [Untitled report submitted to the Violence and Development Project]. New York: Author.

Ngaiza, A. (1989). Tanzania: A life-saving clinic in remote Chanika. In D. De Silva (Project Coordinator), *Against all odds: Breaking the poverty trap* (pp. 27–42). Washington, DC: Panos Institute.

Rohr, J. (1989). Introduction. In J. Rohr (Ed.), *The Third World: Opposing viewpoints* (pp. 12–15). San Diego: Greenhaven Press.

Schiller, B. R. (1989). *The economics of poverty and discrimination*. Englewood Cliffs, NJ: Prentice Hall.

Sherman, A. (1994). *Wasting America's future: The Children's Defense Fund report on the costs of child poverty*. Boston: Beacon Press.

Shuman, M. (1994). *Towards a global village: International community development initiatives*. Boulder, CO: Pluto Press.

UNICEF. (1994). *Progress of Nations 1994*. New York: UNICEF House.

United Nations. (1985). *The United Nations chronicle*. New York: Author.

United Nations. (1995a). *Families: The heart of society* (World Summit for Social Development issue paper). New York: United Nations Department of Public Information.

United Nations. (1995b). *NGOs: Partners in social development* (World Summit for Social Development issue paper). New York: United Nations Department of Public Information.

United Nations. (1995c). *Shelter, employment and the urban poor* (World Summit for Social Development issue paper). New York: United Nations Department of Public Information.

United Nations Development Programme. (1994). *Human development report, 1994*. New York: Oxford University Press.

United Nations Development Programme. (1995). *Human development report, 1995*. New York: Oxford University Press.

U.S. budget for FY '97. (1996). Washington, DC: Office of Management and Budget.

Wines, M., & Pear, R. (1996, July 30). President finds benefits in defeat of health care. *New York Times*, pp. A1, B8.

Yunus, M. (1994). Redefining development. In K. Danaher (Ed.), *50 Years is enough: The case against the World Bank and the International Monetary Fund* (pp. ix–xii). Boston: South End Press.

ADDITIONAL RESOURCES

InterAction: American Council for Voluntary International Action
1717 Massachusetts Avenue, NW, Suite 801
Washington, DC 20036
Phone: 202-667-8227
   An umbrella organization for several hundred international development agencies that address the issue of poverty around the world.

International Council on Social Welfare
380 Saint-Antoine Street West, Suite 3200
Montreal, Quebec, Canada H2Z 3X7
Phone: 514-287-3280; fax: 514-987-1567
   An organization that addresses international social welfare policies and issues and holds an international conference for social welfare professionals.

Oxfam America
26 West Street
Boston, MA 02111
Phone: 617-482-1211
   An international development agency that fights poverty and hunger. It produces educational materials, including videos, and conducts an annual educational campaign, the Fast for a World Harvest.

PART 3

VIOLENCE AGAINST WOMEN AND CHILDREN

CURRICULUM

Part 3 focuses on the pervasive violence against women and children; the impact of this violence at the personal, institutional, and societal levels on sustainable development; and interventions to deal with violence. Strategies that women have used to heal from violence are presented in case studies.

GENERAL OBJECTIVES

1. Students will be able to describe parallel conditions of violence in the United States and in less economically advantaged nations.
2. Students will demonstrate a broadened understanding of violence and the role of the social work profession in solving the problem on a global scale.
3. Students will demonstrate an increased interest in learning from successful interventions undertaken by human services workers in the global South and in the United States.
4. Students will be able to define key concepts, such as sustainable human development, global North, and global South.
5. Students will demonstrate an awareness of social work's commitment to social justice by describing how violence and oppression affect vulnerable populations throughout the world.

The objectives and discussion questions in the following section are presented by curricular area. The questions may be used for classroom discussion or for written assignments. They are based on part 3 of *An Educational Resource* (pp. 55–64

in this volume and pp. 21–30 in the student version).

HUMAN BEHAVIOR IN THE SOCIAL ENVIRONMENT

Objectives

1. Students will demonstrate an understanding of the pervasiveness of both gender violence and violence against children (including forms of violence that are officially sanctioned) as global phenomena that occur both inside and outside the home.
2. Students will demonstrate an understanding that some of the causes of gender violence and violence against children are rooted in the structural relationships of power, domination, and privilege in different societies.
3. Students will be able to define the structure and dynamics of families and cultures that promote violence.
4. Students will demonstrate an understanding of how the threat of male violence is a fundamental experience that unites women across barriers of race, culture, and class throughout the world.
5. Students will demonstrate an understanding that forms of domestic violence can vary depending on specific cultures.
6. Students will demonstrate an understanding of how violence obstructs the healthy development of individuals and societies and how the lack of development opportunities fuels violence.

Discussion Questions

1. What is the impact of violence—at the personal, institutional, and cultural levels—on the development of girls and women throughout the life cycle? Give specific examples.
2. Women and their children are victims of many forms of violence—both inside and outside the home—on a global scale. What are the causes of this prevalent violence?
3. How are refugees, in particular, affected by violence?
4. What are the consequences of gender violence and violence against children for the social and economic development of society?

SOCIAL WORK THEORY AND PRACTICE

Objectives

1. Students will be able to develop new practice models and strategies that are based on methods and strategies that have been developed in different countries to empower women, challenge unequal gender relations, and stop violence.
2. Students will be able to explicate the steps necessary to bring about sustainable human and social development as an antidote to violence.
3. Students will have a wider frame of reference from which to assess the needs and capacities of families and opportunities for the peaceful resolution of conflicts.
4. Students will expand their practice skills in mediation and the de-escalation of violence.
5. Students will contribute to community-based and macrolevel practice interventions, using global models.

Discussion Questions

1. Social workers often work with families in which violence (battering, child abuse, and incest) is an issue. What are the implications for practice of expanding the analysis of domestic violence as a problem that is "not just a family affair"? What new strategies would be suggested?
2. *An Educational Resource* (p. 56 in this volume and p. 22 in the student version) presents examples of violence against children that are

not usually considered to be child abuse. What are some of these forms of violence, and what impact, if any, would they have on the practice of U.S. social workers?
3. In working with refugee women and children, what are some of the factors that should be considered when assessing their situations?

SOCIAL WELFARE POLICY

Objectives

1. Students will demonstrate an understanding of violence by men against women as a social and economic development issue.
2. Students will be able to define policies on various levels that contribute to violence and obstruct development.
3. Students will be able to describe approaches to sustainable human development that address the problems of gender violence and violence against children.

Discussion Questions

1. What does sustainable human development mean? How can it be an antidote to gender violence?
2. Much has been written about how social and economic development approaches have resulted in increased rates of gender violence. What policies and program issues need to be addressed to prevent such an increase?
3. What are the implications of international conferences, such as the Fourth World Conference on Women, held in Beijing in September 1995, for social welfare policy in the United States?
4. Why is wife beating a social and economic development issue?

RESEARCH

Objectives

1. Students will draw on international qualitative and quantitative data to make sense of social and economic injustice in the United States.
2. Students will demonstrate an understanding of the importance of gathering data globally

to compare the situations of women and children (for example, in relation to women's employment rights and the rights of children) in various countries.

Discussion Questions

1. What research evidence is there to support the contention that gender violence and violence against children are global problems?
2. Choose an arena of violence that you want to learn more about on an international scale, such as the sex tourism industry, women as political prisoners, or child abuse in the home. How would you approach doing research in that area?
3. In part 3 of *An Educational Resource* (pp. 57–58 in this volume and pp. 23–25 in the student version) describes several links between violence and development (for example, the effect of domestic violence on children's development). How would you approach doing research on the links between gender violence and violence against children and development?

FIELD PRACTICUM

Objectives

1. Students will identify and understand models of community organizing in a variety of countries.
2. Students will define levels of intervention in context, including the effect of environments on all people.
3. Students will define advocacy skills and apply them in their agencies and wider community.
4. Students will share their international experiences gained either through travel or from interviews with people from other countries.

Discussion Questions

1. Does gender violence affect clients in your field placement? If so, how? Are the conditions described in part 3 of *An Educational Resource* (pp. 55–56 in this volume and pp. 21–22 in the student version) relevant for your field practice? If so, how?

2. Does violence against children affect clients in your field placement? If so, how? Are the conditions described in part 3 of *An Educational Resource* (p. 56 in this volume and p. 22 in the student version) relevant for your field practice with children? If so, how?
3. What relevance, if any, does the experience of the women of Annapurna Mahila Mandal (described in part 3 of *An Educational Resource*, pp. 61–62 in this volume and pp. 27–28 of the student version) have for your field practice?

Case Study
Women Healing from Violence in Nicaragua

Ask the students to read the case study in part 3 of *An Educational Resource* (p. 61 in this volume and p. 27 in the student volume).

Discussion Questions

1. What steps and skills did the women use to resolve their conflicts?
2. What were the key factors that led to healing?
3. What are the connections between violence and development in this story?
4. What universal information may be gained from the story?
5. What are the implications for social work practice in the United States?

Case Study
Linking Family Structure with Violence and the Prevention of Violence in Kerala, India

Ask the students to read the case study in part 3 of *An Educational Resource* (pp. 61–62 in this volume and pp. 27–28 in the student version).

Discussion Questions

1. What alternatives (including social and economic options) do women have for dealing with their situations?
2. What family resources are there to support women's choices?

3. How could societies and cultures be more sensitive and supportive of the needs of families?
4. What are the advantages and disadvantages of various grassroots initiatives (for example, women organizing to promote their rights) compared with the development of state and national policies?
5. How could social and human development strategies alleviate patriarchy and become sustainable?
6. What are the implications and applicability of the approaches taken in Kerala for social work intervention in the United States?

Exercise 1—Writing Assignment
Developing an Intervention Plan to Address Family Violence

Purpose

To assess a specific case situation involving violence and outline a plan of intervention.

Learning Activity

Have the students identify a specific family case situation in which violence has occurred, is occurring, or has the potential to occur. When possible, students should use cases with which they are familiar in their practice or field internships, although they can also use hypothetical cases. Assign a three-part paper about the case situation that includes the following:
- definitions of the structural and dynamic variables in the family and the culture that contribute to the occurrence of violence
- a plan for intervention that includes sustainable human and social development from the micro (family) level to the macro (social policy) level nationally and internationally
- indicators of the effectiveness of the interventions.

Source: Developed by Dr. Allie Kilpatrick, School of Social Work, University of Georgia, Athens.

Exercise 2—Writing Assignment
Position Paper on Raising the Status of Women

Purpose

To analyze two arguments that are made for raising the status of women and to articulate one's own position.

Learning Activity

Ask the students to read the arguments for raising the status of women in part 3 of *An Educational Resource* (p. 58 in this volume and p. 24 in the student version) and then to write papers in which they do all of the following:
1. List at least one example of an approach to raising the status of women that is based on the equity argument. Describe the approach and the rationale given for the approach and document all sources.
2. List at least one example of an approach to raising the status of women that is based on the efficiency argument. Describe the approach and rationale given for the approach and document all sources.
3. Discuss why governments and other development agencies often use efficiency arguments, rather than equity arguments, for enhancing the status of women and including them in development.
4. Discuss which argument—the equity argument or the efficiency argument—you feel most strongly about when advocating for raising the status of women and tell why.

Source: Adapted from a discussion handout in Gross, 1993.

Exercise 3—Gender Analysis

Purpose

To conduct a gender analysis of a community or a society.

Learning Activity

Each student should select for analysis a community with which he or she is familiar—either a neighborhood, city, or county in the United States or a country of origin if the student is from another country. The analysis should be based on answers to the following questions, and sources should be documented throughout.

1. Who does what? The issue to be addressed is the actual (as opposed to the idealized) division of labor between men and women in the community being analyzed.
2. Who has what? The issue to be addressed is who has access to, and control over, private resources in this community.
3. What factors influence this gender arrangement? The issue to be addressed is which factors—cultural prescriptions, law, economic policy, and political policy—influence this gender arrangement, if they are changing and how, and which are manipulable.
4. How are public resources distributed, and who gets what? What institutional structures are used? How equitable are they? How efficient? What can be done to make them more responsive to women as well as men? These questions can produce different answers, depending on the country, sector, institutions, and other contextual factors.
5. Recommendations for change. On the basis of your answers to the foregoing questions, what recommendations would you make for improving the status of women in the particular community?

REFERENCE

Gross, S. H. (1993). *How-to-do-it manual: Ideas for teaching about contemporary women in Africa, Asia, and Latin America.* (Available from the Upper Midwest Women's History Center, 6300 Walker St., St. Louis Park, MN 55416)

FOR FURTHER READING

Carrillo, R. (1992). *Battered dreams: Violence against women as an obstacle to development.* New York: United Nations Development Fund for Women.

This book links gender-based violence to development, on the thesis that development plans cannot succeed if they ignore the reality that gender-based violence hinders women's participation in the process at many levels. It presents useful direction for programs and policy and includes a comprehensive section on resources.

Center for Battered Women. (n.d.). *Expect respect: A curriculum of the Teen Dating Violence Project.* Austin, TX: Author.

Manuals that offer guidance in forming peer-support groups and conducting educational presentations for young men and women on how to prevent violence (Available from the center at P.O. Box 19454, Austin, TX 78760; phone 512-385-5181, fax 512-385-0662)

Davies, M. (1994). *Women and violence: Realities and responses worldwide.* Atlantic Highlands, NJ: Zed Books.

This book is an anthology of the universality of gender violence through the experiences and analyses of individual women and women's groups in 30 countries. Its premise is that violence against women is rooted in the structural relationships of power, domination, and between women and men in different societies. Some of the root causes and effective strategies for change that women are attempting to develop are explored.

McFadden, E. J. (Ed.). (1991). *Child welfare around the world.* Washington, DC: Child Welfare League of America.

The aims of this sampler of information on child welfare throughout the world are to facilitate the reciprocal transfer of knowledge among nations; to broaden understanding of the ways in which child welfare practice is shaped by social, economic, and political processes, as well as by racism, sexism, and the legacy of colonialism; and to further a global perspective on the urgent survival needs of children.

Wetzel, J. W. (1993). *The world of women: In pursuit of human rights*. New York: New York University Press.

This book examines the social issues and problems that affect women throughout the world, the policies and practices that impinge on women's human rights, and the various programs that have been successful in changing women's conditions. It takes an interdisciplinary approach that links discrimination and violence against women to family law; sex roles to sex industries; and sexual oppression to politics, education, employment, health, and mental health.

Young, G., Samarasinghe, V., & Kusterer, K. (Eds.). (1993). *Women at the center: Development issues and practices for the 1990s*. West Hartford, CT: Kumarian Press.

This review and synthesis of current scholarly thinking, policy practice, and activists' experiences in relation to women and development are based on several assumptions. These assumptions are that the struggle for development and gender equity is global, sought everywhere yet achieved nowhere; that policymakers, activists, and scholars can all learn from one another's knowledge and experience; that people who are working in the global North have much to learn from people working in the global South, and vice versa; and that lessons learned from the experiences gained in one field can help those who are working for development and empowerment in other fields.

CHAPTER 3-2

VIOLENCE AGAINST WOMEN AND CHILDREN

EDUCATIONAL RESOURCE

Violence within the context of the family is a social problem with which the social work profession has been deeply concerned. However, violence against women and children does not occur in the isolation of the home. Rather, it is deeply embedded in a global ideology of male superiority that makes women and children particularly vulnerable to violence in all domains.

Violence against women worldwide is pervasive and serious, yet the problem was denied for a long time. According to the World-Watch Institute (Heise, 1989), "Violence against wives, indeed violence against [females] in general, is as old as recorded history, and cuts across all societies and socioeconomic groups. There are few phenomena so pervasive and yet so ignored" (p. 12).

The issue of violence within the family was first raised as a serious concern in 1975 at the International Women's Year World Conference in Mexico City (United Nations [UN], 1975a, 1975b). However, it was not until the 1980 Mid-Decade World Conference for Women in Copenhagen that the need to eliminate all forms of violence against women was fully recognized, and the Convention on the Elimination of All Forms of Discrimination Against Women was endorsed (UN, 1980).

Gender violence became a prominent issue at the 1985 World Conference on Women in Nairobi (UN, 1985). For the first time, women came together as activists for change within the international community. Violence against women is now considered "a serious issue and the subject of worldwide debate. The problem has been recognized as a serious obstacle to development and peace" (UN, 1989b, p. 3).

The rights of children also received international recognition with the passage of the Declaration on the Rights of the Child by the UN General Assembly in November 1989 (UN, 1989a). The declaration calls on nations to protect children from all forms of violence and exploitation.

Part 3 explores the pervasiveness of violence against women and children. It examines how violence obstructs the healthy development of individuals and societies and how the lack of development opportunities fuels violence and discusses what has been done and what still needs to be done to prevent violence against women.

GENDER VIOLENCE: A GLOBAL PROBLEM

Much of the violence that is directed toward women is rooted in economic, political, cultural, and religious systems that ensure male domination and control. Because violence against women is normalized to such a large extent, it is not considered unusual behavior when women are murdered, assaulted, sexually abused, threatened, or humiliated by their male partners (UN, 1989b). Traditions and social systems legitimate gender discrimination beginning at birth (Anderson & Moore, 1993).

Although the various dimensions of violence against women throughout the world have not been sufficiently documented, the following statistics shed light on its pervasiveness:

- In the United States, battery is the leading cause of injury to adult women (Koop, 1989).
- Domestic violence is estimated to occur in at least 70 percent of Mexican families (Carrillo, 1991).
- In Pakistan, at least one woman is burned alive by her husband each day, and there are many more cases that go unreported (Sennott, 1995).
- There are 100 million fewer females in Asia than would have been produced by normal birthrates owing to female infanticide, selective feeding of infants, and selective abortion practices (Clifton, 1995).
- The UN estimated that two out of three of the world's unschooled, and thus illiterate, people are female (Minnesota NASW chapter Center, 1994).

The widespread cultural belief that women are inferior gives rise to inequity, which in itself is a form of violence. In the global South, girls are more likely than are boys to be given less food, denied access to education and health care, forced into hard labor sooner, denied any kind of economic return on their labor, made to marry as young teenagers, bought and sold like slaves for prostitution and labor, and killed by sex-selective abortions and female infanticide (Minnesota NASW chapter Center, 1994).

Women also suffer from additional forms of violence that are officially sanctioned:

- Many of the world's political prisoners are women activists who have spoken out against gender-based violence.
- More women than men die as a result of armed conflicts.
- The majority of women do not enjoy basic human and civil rights in many countries. Although some countries have laws against gender inequity, these laws are often not enforced (Minnesota NASW chapter Center, 1994).
- Women still earn 30 percent to 40 percent less than do their male counterparts for comparable work (*Hunger 1995*, 1995).

VIOLENCE AGAINST CHILDREN

Like women, children are victims of many forms of violence, both inside and outside the home. According to Childhelp USA, one in three girls and one in eight boys are sexually abused in the United States before age 18 (Rohr, 1990). The majority of child sexual abuse in this country is perpetrated by someone known to the children—usually their fathers, stepfathers, or father substitutes. Although there is limited information about family sexual abuse in the global South, studies done in the Philippines, Sri Lanka, and Thailand suggest that the extent of the problem is similar to that of the United States (Centre for Protection of Children's Rights, 1991; Doek, 1991).

Another form of child abuse that has gained notoriety in recent years is the selling of children for sex to tourists and other international visitors in Asian, African, and Latin American countries. Children are also involved in prostitution in disturbingly large numbers in Western Europe and North America, and there are reports of a growth in child sexual exploitation in the former Communist countries of Eastern Europe. The perpetrators are almost always male, whereas the children who are exploited are both male and female—although girls constitute by far the greatest proportion of the victims (Ireland, 1993).

The following quotation illustrates the magnitude of violence against children worldwide:

> The stories pour forth in an avalanche of horror. From Bosnia, young girls raped . . . and murdered. From Angola, Cambodia, Afghanistan, Mozambique, children literally torn to shreds by land-mines. . . . From Brazil, a paramilitary massacre of street children while they sleep in the quiet shadows of a church. From Thailand, young girls, stolen from their Myanmar villages, to be locked in brothels, servicing male sexual predators. From Somalia, Sudan, Rwanda, child refugees on the run . . . fleeing civil war, cut down in their flight by mortars, bullets, machetes. (UNICEF, 1994)

OBSTACLES TO DEVELOPMENT

Male Domination

A faith in violence as a solution to problems and militaristic values at the structural level results in boys being programmed to assume roles of dominance and male supremacy. There seems to be a connection between this culturally programmed desire for dominance and the fact that so many men around the world turn to violence against women (Pogrebin, 1990). The low economic position of women (and children) is linked with their vulnerability to violence, particularly in their households. The subordination of women in society allows them to be victims of violence. "Violence against women is a function of the belief, fostered in all cultures, that men are superior and that the women they live with are their possessions or chattels that they can treat as they wish and as they consider appropriate" (UN, 1989b, p. 33).

Militarism

> Left to sustain the family and endure the loneliness and vulnerability of separation, women suffer great hardships in wartime. Their houses may be damaged, or they may flee from home for fear of their lives. Dwindling food supplies and hungry children exacerbate tensions. And so, to the loss of husbands, fathers, sons and brothers who are killed in battle, is added the suffering of further deprivation. Often defenseless against invasion, women can find that armed conflict means rape and other forms of abuse by occupying troops, as well as a loss of the means of livelihood. (Vickers, 1993, p. 18)

Women are affected by war in a multitude of ways:

- In 1992, more people were killed in wars than at any time throughout the Cold War. Women and children were the primary victims of those wars (Sivard, 1993).
- Women are extremely vulnerable to rape, torture, and exploitation during military conflicts. There is growing international recognition that rape is being used as a tactic or prize of war (UN Development Programme, 1994).

- Of the people who are killed by antipersonnel mines, 30 percent to 40 percent are women and children (UN Development Programme, 1994).
- Of the world's refugees, 80 percent are women and their dependent children (*Hunger 1995*, 1995).
- As of 1994, approximately 200,000 children had been recruited to be soldiers. These children have been separated from their families, denied a normal life, subjected to military training that has distorted their values, and traumatized by war experiences (*Children at War*, 1994; InterAction, 1994).

In addition, unprecedented military spending in both the global North and the global South since the 1970s has slowed progress in the areas of health, education, and other basic needs in many parts of the world. This lack of progress has adversely affected the health and status of women and has made it difficult for poor women to get the services they need for themselves and their children (Sivard, 1993).

Domestic Violence

Domestic violence is a form of control that puts women's health—and lives—at risk, denies them their human rights, and hinders their full participation in society. For example, case studies of victims of domestic violence in Peru and Mexico revealed that men frequently beat their wives to demand the income these women had earned (Vasquez & Tamayo, 1989). A project of the Working Women's Forum in Madras, India, almost collapsed when the most articulate and energetic women started to drop out because of increasing domestic violence against them as a result of their involvement in the project (Carrillo, 1992).

Domestic violence also affects children's development. A Canadian study reported high incidences of posttraumatic stress disorder, clinical dysfunction, and behavioral and emotional disorders in children from violent homes (Jaffe, Wilson, & Wolfe, 1986).

Unfortunately, the institutional response to family violence is often inadequate. Almost universally, the social impulse is to preserve the family at all costs, even if doing so compromises a woman's safety. As a high court judge in Uganda expressed, "It is better for one person to suffer rather than risk a complete breakdown of family life" (Heise, 1989, p. 13).

Changing Political and Economic Systems

Political and economic changes that affect poor people frequently lead to the disruption of traditional ways of life and hence cause social norms and established means of providing for the community to unravel. In addition to the breakdown in old systems, adequate alternatives are rarely in place to support people's needs. These desperate circumstances create conditions of "every man for himself." In the process, women and children often emerge as the most vulnerable (UN, 1989b; personal correspondence between Violence & Development Project and K. Kusterer, March 18, 1995).

One example of this problem is the worldwide trend toward the urbanization of rural peoples after their traditional ways of life have been disrupted by outside influences. Rapid urbanization and migration result in underemployment and underdevelopment, including the lack of access to basic resources and services. In such situations, a precarious economic existence is inevitable, and in people's struggle to survive, violence is often a result (Wetzel, 1993).

Absence of Development Opportunities

Underdevelopment, juxtaposed with a fiercely materialistic culture, feeds violence in the United States. It has been suggested that increasing violence is the result of "the sullen rage of mostly boys and young men who live in poverty and are taunted by visions of affluence and ease which they have no hope of reaching" (Washington Spectator, 1990, p. 171).

Inadequate development also seems to be a significant cause of violence in the lives of children in the global South. For example, nearly all Latin America's street children, 10 percent to 30 percent of whom are female, are engaged in some form of economic activity on the streets to sup-

port themselves or to supplement their families' incomes. Many report feeling proud to bring their earnings home to their families. Seventy-five percent of the girls on Latin America's streets are there to help meet their family's economic needs, with their parents' blessing (Rizzini & Lusk, 1995). However, living on the streets makes children vulnerable to prostitution, drug abuse, violence, and death. On average, six street children in Columbia and four in Brazil are killed each day (Castilho, 1995).

WHY RAISE THE STATUS OF WOMEN?

Basically, two arguments are made for raising the status of women; providing girls and women with more opportunities; and eliminating harmful customs against girls and women, such as the preference, of parents in some cultures, for having boys: the equity argument and the efficiency argument. The equity argument claims that it is unfair to women and girls when resources are distributed or withheld on the basis of sex, when women are not given equal educational and work opportunities, and when women's human rights are violated.

The efficiency argument claims that improving the status of girls and women will allow women to be part of the economic and social development of their countries and, therefore, will benefit everyone. This argument claims that it is inefficient and wasteful not to include women in development programs and points to studies that have found that women who have incomes spend their money to improve the lives of their children and communities more than do men. Thus, development progresses faster (Gross, 1993).

SUSTAINABLE HUMAN DEVELOPMENT: AN ANTIDOTE TO VIOLENCE AGAINST WOMEN AND CHILDREN

Many of the development issues that affect woman and children are the same in both the United States and the global South: violence in the home, community, and society at large; the absence of public money or the commitment to address social problems; low wages; and the lack of access to economic opportunities. To address these problems, two approaches have been suggested.

Gender-Sensitive Development

Development experts have come to realize that investing in women is the surest way to improve life for all because women have the primary responsibility for the well-being of the family and the community (*Hunger 1995*, 1995). Tisch and Wallace (1994) suggested that a gender analysis should be integrated into the conception, design, and implementation of all development projects. Such an analysis would take into account the impact of a project on women's and men's roles and responsibilities.

Development initiatives should involve women at every stage of planning and execution to ensure that their perspective and needs are fully accounted for (Tisch & Wallace, 1994). Far too often, projects are designed without consulting women, with the result that sometimes the amount of work they are required to do is increased. For example, when improved plowing techniques were introduced in Kenya, male farmers were able to double the number of acres they could plant. The project, however, also doubled the already taxing workload of women, because traditionally it was the women's job to weed the fields—by hand (*Hunger 1995*, 1995).

The following recommendations, proposed by the International Center for Research on Women (1993), are designed to promote gender-sensitive development:

- develop economic opportunities for women in private enterprise, in agriculture, and all sectors of formal employment
- close the gender gap in literacy and education
- increase women's reproductive choices by providing accessible, high-quality health and family planning services
- ensure that development efforts balance long-term environmental sustainability and women's subsistence and economic needs based on natural resources

- ensure that emergency and development assistance programs take into account women's roles, needs, and human rights in times of conflict, famine, disease, and rapidly changing economic and political circumstances.

Development That Addresses Violence against Women

As Heise (as quoted in Carrillo, 1991) noted:

> The development community has come to realize that problems such as high fertility, deforestation and hunger cannot be solved without women's full participation. Yet, women cannot lend their labor or creative ideas fully when they are burdened with the physical and psychological scars of violence. (p. 11)

It is clear that attempts to integrate women into development are doomed to failure if they do not make violence against women the central issue (Women's Feature Service, 1993). Development agencies can make an important contribution by documenting the obstacles that gender violence places in the path of development and by identifying strategies for countering them. Carrillo (1992) argued that the development community should support projects that address gender violence as legitimate projects in themselves. Some efforts that have been made to counter violence against women include these:

- In Bombay, "ladies-only" cars were set aside in the mass transit system to prevent women from being harassed by men as they traveled to work (Carrillo, 1992).
- In Tempoal, Mexico, staff at the United Nations Development Fund for Women project worked with husbands and other members of the community to address the increased violence that emerged as a result of women's changing roles (Carrillo, 1992).
- In Cambodia, where efforts are under way to rebuild the nation after many years of war, a study was conducted to assess the legal rights of Cambodian women and the prevalence of domestic violence (study by the Asia Foundation, reported in an interview with Kathy Zimmerman on *All Things Considered*, 1995).

CASE STUDIES

The following case studies provide inspiring accounts of how women in Nicaragua and in two regions of India are not only finding ways to heal from trauma but are becoming empowered to take control of their lives.

CASE STUDY 1
Women Healing from Violence in Nicaragua

San Pablo del Norte (a fictitious name), a small town in the northern mountains of Nicaragua, may seem quiet enough now, but in the 1980s it was the object of several Contra attacks. Although many families had sons and siblings who were fighting on opposing sides of the civil war, no one ever talked much about the divisions that might have been caused. The Contra sympathizers went to military camps in Honduras, and the families they left behind kept silent about the ones who had clearly chosen another path.

After the war officially ended, the Contras euphorically returned home, many of them with their families. Their sense of euphoria was short-lived, however, as they restlessly and resentfully looked for land to farm (there was none) and a way to survive. Most of the tools and building materials promised by the government in exchange for weapons never arrived. Families who had been silent about their divisions during the war were now publicly splitting apart; whole communities became polarized.

Even the women, whose interest in politics was minimal (they primarily cared about food, clothing, and shelter for their loved ones), were affected by ruptures in the community. Each woman was identified by the side her husband had taken. There were angry quarrels, ugly rumors, and rampant distrust.

This was the situation that faced two women who came to San Juan del Norte as representatives of the Nicaraguan Network for the Promotion of Mental Health. Their intention was to help the women of the town to understand that they had human rights and that they could organize—beginning with mutual help and support groups—to find ways to improve their lives and those of their children.

This was no easy task. Even after the women agreed to meet, they stared at each other with anger, remembering the unspeakable harm done by the war, and refused to speak. Weeks and months later, the silence was broken, when little by little the women began to speak pieces of their truth more openly. The women continued to stare at each other, but now in amazement at their common stories. In time, the stories came pouring out like rivers in full flood: tales of hunger, death, and sickness and nothing to give the children; tales of unending grief for fallen loves ones and the land that once was their home; and tales of bitter—sometimes murderous—hatred between brothers. The women moved closer together, huddling against the cruelty and chaos of the outside world to comfort one another in what they now recognized as their common misery and pain.

Despite recurring waves of distrust and disagreement in their groups, the women found they could work together collectively for their common good. Realizing that they shared a common grief was the glue that bound them together. Thus, they found solace in one another. They learned to trust each other enough to work in small cooperatives to improve the economic status of their families.

One *campesina* (woman farmworker), with work-worn hands and lines of sorrow etched in her face, stated with certainty and quiet pride, "It is men who make war. We women are the ones who know how to reconcile, to make peace" (case study contributed by Constance Fabunmi, Minnesota NASW chapter Center on Violence, Development, and Family Structure; used with permission of the author).

CASE STUDY 2
Kerala, India: Linking Family Structure with Violence and Violence Prevention

Several Christian religious orders are working to meet the needs of people in cities and villages throughout the state of Kerala by, for example, setting up hospice programs; homes for the elderly; and educational, counseling, and advocacy programs. One order, the Carmellite sisters, has initiated a combined program of education and advocacy for women that has been highly successful and may well be viewed as feminism at its best.

The Carmellite nuns have approached the issue of equal status for women with a two-pronged plan: instituting special courses for women in the educational institutions run by their order and providing individual advocacy on behalf of women who have been abused, violated, or mistreated.

The first line of defense is to educate women about their self-worth and intrinsic value as human beings who have both human and legal rights. For many women, these awareness-raising classes are their first exposure to this philosophy. When women become empowered to value themselves, the first step toward the prevention of violence has been taken. Subsequently, these women are provided with information about specific legal rights.

The Carmellite nuns have also developed a program of individual advocacy to combat specific occurrences of abuse and other forms of violence whenever and wherever it occurs. For example, a member of the religious community will go with a woman who is facing a particular trauma and intercede on her behalf with her accuser—opponent—often a government official or employee in the public sector. This action frequently involves making court appearances and interceding with judges or going to police stations and taking a stand with male police officers. The result of this intervention is that government officials listen to the woman and give her a "fair" hearing, whereas previously her testimony or viewpoint would have probably been ignored. Such advocacy is not always approached from a defensive posture; frequently, the nuns take an offensive position and help a woman initiate a needed action (such as obtaining child support payments from a deserting husband). Many favorable outcomes have been obtained through this process.

It is incredible that a male-oriented, Hindu-dominated society would tolerate such aggressive action by the nuns. One reason for the success of the program is that Kerala has a strong tradition of respect for individual religious rights. Another reason is that religious people (nuns, priests, and other clergy and gurus) are held in high regard. The populace is virtually in awe of the nuns. The order's schools are the best in Kerala, and it is

considered highly desirable to attend them. Furthermore, the nuns are respected because in addition to their religious affiliation, they have the worldliness to operate major educational institutions successfully. Thus, their actions and words are perceived as credible. The Carmellites look forward to the day when the family structure in India will reflect equal human rights for all family members, including women and girls, and they can focus their efforts on prevention, rather than intervention (case study contributed by Marilyn J. Kennedy, Minnesota NASW chapter Center on Violence, Development, and Family Structure; used with permission of the author).

CASE STUDY 3

Annapurna Mahila Mandal: A Triumph of Women's Strength

In India, thousands of men pour into Bombay from the surrounding countryside to work in the city's thriving textile mills. In the poor neighborhoods (known as the *busti*) where the workers live, enterprising women have developed small catering businesses to feed the men. Along with exhausting workloads, these women contend with chronic indebtedness; they are forced to buy grains and other provisions on credit—often at annual interest rates of over 100 percent (*Update India*, 1991).

To address some of these problems, 14 determined women founded a small organization in 1973 that they aptly named Annapurna Mahila Mandal, after the Hindu goddess of food. For almost 10 years, Annapurna operated entirely on volunteer labor and donated space and money. Then, in 1982, with help from international development agencies, it opened a multipurpose facility with paid staff to support its expanding program: loan services, a medical clinic, legal counseling, and vocational skills training.

Thousands of members of Annapurna have since borrowed millions of rupees from a revolving loan fund that boasts an almost perfect repayment record. By providing women caterers with capital support, equipment, and training, the organization has liberated its members from exploitative money lenders. Now that their catering businesses are more secure, women have become free to tackle new challenges: campaigning against dowries, domestic violence, and other discriminatory laws and practices.

Annapurna has been so successful that it has expanded its operations to Vashi, on the outskirts of Bombay. In addition to catering food for nearby factories and offices, the Vashi center provides a temporary home to women who are destitute, abused, or abandoned by their husbands.

One of Annapurna's most important contributions is instilling a sense of dignity in women. Prema Purao, one of the founders of Annapurna, tells the women: "Your work is important and worthy of pride" (*Update India*, 1991, p. 4). By changing the way women think about themselves, Annapurna is improving the lives of extended families and entire communities.

WHAT YOU CAN DO

- Learn what women's groups are doing in countries of the global South to stop violence and promote development.
- Advocate to increase the number of women in leadership positions in the United Nations, international development organizations, and U.S. development projects.
- Read about the outcomes of the Fourth UN World Conference on Women, held in Beijing, China, in September 1995 (see, for example, UN, 1995).
- Advocate for the increased availability of child care services and health insurance for workers and for laws and regulations that prohibit gender discrimination.
- Remember that early attitudes about gender roles and gender violence are shaped in school. Therefore, ensure that children are taught that violence against women is unacceptable and that sexual harassment and abuse in the schools will not be tolerated.

REFERENCES

All things considered. (1995, August 31). Interview with Kathy Zimmerman. [Study funded by Asia Foundation, 465 California Street, San Francisco, CA 94105; phone 415-982-4640]. Washington, DC: National Public Radio.

Anderson, J., & Moore, M. (1993, February 14–18). Born oppressed: Women in the developing world face cradle to grave discrimination, poverty. *Washington Post*, pp. 1–6.

Carrillo, R. (1991). Violence against women: An obstacle to development. In Center for Women's Global Leadership, *Gender violence: A development and human rights issue* (pp. 19–41). Highland Park, NJ: Plowshares Press.

Carrillo, R. (1992). *Battered dreams: Violence against women as an obstacle to development.* New York: United Nations Development Fund for Women.

Castilho, C. (1995, January). Children to the slaughter: Street life is deadly in Latin American countries. *World Paper*, p. 12.

Centre for Protection of Children's Rights. (1991). *Report on child rights violations: Annual report to 31 December 1991.* Bangkok, Thailand: Author.

Children at war. (1994). (Available from Save the Children, 52 Wilton Road, Westport, CT 06880; phone 203-221-4000)

Clifton, T. (1995, August 25). Asia's disappearing girls. *Minneapolis Star Tribune*, p. 16A.

Doek, J. E. (1991). Management of child abuse and neglect at the international level: Trends and perspectives. *Child Abuse and Neglect, 15*(1), 51–56.

Gross, S. H. (1993). *How-to-do-it manual: Ideas for teaching about contemporary women in Africa, Asia, and Latin America.* St. Louis Park, MN: Upper Midwest Women's History Center.

Heise, L. (1989, March–April). Crimes of gender. *World Watch*, pp. 12–21.

Hunger 1995: Causes of hunger. (1995). (Available from Bread for the World Institute, 1100 Wayne Avenue South, Suite 1000, Silver Spring, MD 20910; phone 301-608-2400)

InterAction. (1994, July 18). Strategies for families in war zones in Africa. *Monday Developments, 12,* 13. (Available from InterAction, 1717 Massachusetts Avenue, NW, Suite 801, Washington, DC 20036; phone 202-667-8227)

International Center for Research on Women. (1993, February 19). *Women's issues in development cooperation: A call for action.* (Available from the Center at 1717 Massachusetts Avenue, NW, Suite 302, Washington, DC 20036; phone 202-797-0007)

Ireland, K. (1993, September). *Wish you weren't here: The sexual exploitation of children and the connection with tourism and international travel* (Working Paper No. 7). (Available from the Overseas Department, Save the Children, 52 Wilton Road, Westport, CT 06880; phone 203-221-4000)

Jaffe, P., Wilson, S., & Wolfe, D. A. (1986). Promoting changes in attitudes and understanding of conflict resolution among child witnesses of family violence. *Canadian Journal of Behavioral Science, 18,* 356.

Koop, C. E. (1989). *Violence against women: A global problem.* Presentation by the Surgeon General of the United States to the U.S. Public Health Service. Washington, DC: U.S. Government Printing Office.

Minnesota NASW chapter Center on Violence, Development, and Family Structure. (1994). *Analysis of the linkages between violence and development/underdevelopment within the context of family structure* (Report submitted to the Violence and Development Project). St. Paul, MN: Author.

Pogrebin, L. C. (1990). Restrictive gender roles create teen rapists. In J. Rohr (Ed.), *Violence in America: Opposing viewpoints* (pp. 187–190). San Diego: Greenhaven Press.

Rizzini, I., & Lusk, M. (1995). Children in the streets: Latin America's lost generation. *Children and Youth Services Review, 17(3),* 387–395.

Rohr, J. (Ed.). (1990). Introduction. In J. Rohr (Ed.), *Violence in America: Opposing viewpoints* (pp. 12–15). San Diego: Greenhaven Press.

Sennott, C. (1995, May 18). Rights groups battle burning of women in Pakistan. *Boston Globe,* p. 1.

Sivard, R. L. (1993). *World military and social expenditures 1993.* Washington, DC: World Priorities.

Tisch, S. J., & Wallace, M. B. (1994). *Dilemmas of development assistance: The what, why, and who of foreign aid.* Boulder, CO: Westview Press.

UNICEF. (1994). *Progress of nations 1994.* New York: UNICEF House, p. 37.

United Nations. (1975a). *Declaration of Mexico City: Report of the international women's year world conference, Mexico City, Mexico.* New York: Author.

United Nations. (1975b). *World plan of action: Report of the international women's year world conference, Mexico City, Mexico.* New York: Author.

United Nations. (1980). *Convention on the elimination of all forms of discrimination against women: Report of the mid-decade world conference for women, Copenhagen, Denmark.* New York: Author.

United Nations. (1985). *Nairobi forward-looking strategies for the advancement of women: Report of the end of decade world conference on women.* New York: Author.

United Nations. (1989a). *Declaration on the rights of the child.* New York: Author.

United Nations. (1989b). *Violence against women in the family.* New York: Author.

United Nations. (1995). *Platform for action: Report of the Fourth World Conference on Women, Beijing, China.* New York: Author.

United Nations Development Programme. (1994). *Human development report, 1994.* New York: Oxford University Press.

Update: India. (1991). (Available from Oxfam America, 26 West Street, Boston, MA 02111)

Vasquez, S. R., & Tamayo, L. G. (1989, May). *Violencia y legalidad.* Lima, Peru: CONCYTEC.

Vickers, J. (1993). *Women and war.* Atlantic Highlands, NJ: Zed Books.

Washington Spectator. (1990). Poverty promotes teen violence. In J. Rohr (Ed.)., *Violence in America: Opposing viewpoints* (pp. 170–175). San Diego: Greenhaven Press.

Wetzel, J. W. (1993). *The world of women: In pursuit of human rights*. New York: New York University Press.

Women's Feature Service. (1993). *The power to change: Women in the Third World redefine their environment*. Atlantic Highlands, NJ: Zed Books.

ADDITIONAL RESOURCES

Association for Women in Development
1511 K Street, NW, Suite 825
Washington, DC 20005
Phone: 202-628-0440

An organization that works to define development based on women's perspectives and promotes research, policy, and practice to engage women fully in building a just and sustainable development process.

Center for Women's Global Leadership
Douglass College, Rutgers University
27 Clifton Avenue
New Brunswick, NJ 08903-0270
Phone: 908-932-8782

A center that works to shape and advance women's rights and is helping to build the women's international human rights network.

Women's Commission for Refugee Women
and Children
International Rescue Committee
122 East 42nd Street
New York, NY 10016-1289
Phone: 212-551-3086

An advocacy and expert-resource organization that deals with issues facing uprooted women and children. It sends delegations to refugee settings that observe and make recommendations for improving conditions and provides an educational program for high school teachers and students about the experience of refugees.

PART 4

CHAPTER 4-1

ETHNICITY

CURRICULUM

Part 4 explores some of the various causes and consequences of racial and ethnic conflict around the world, the types of hate crimes, and the connection between the lack of development opportunities and unjust development and ethnoviolence. Case studies illustrate the types of hate crimes and strategies that have been used to resolve conflict.

GENERAL OBJECTIVES

1. Students will be able to describe parallel conditions of violence in the United States and in less economically advantaged nations.
2. Students will demonstrate a broadened understanding of violence and the role of the social work profession in solving the problem on a global scale.
3. Students will demonstrate an increased interest in learning from successful interventions by human services workers in the global South and in the United States.
4. Students will be able to define key concepts, such as sustainable human development, global North, and global South.
5. Students will demonstrate an awareness of social work's commitment to social justice by describing how violence and oppression affect vulnerable populations worldwide.

The objectives and discussion questions in the following section are presented by curriculum area. The questions may be used for classroom discussion or in written assignments. They are based on information presented in part 4 of *An*

Educational Resource (pp. 77–83 in this volume and pp. 31–37 in the student version).

HUMAN BEHAVIOR IN THE SOCIAL ENVIRONMENT

Objectives

1. Students will demonstrate an understanding of the common causes and consequences of racial and ethnic conflict in the United States and in the global South.
2. Students will describe various connections between ethnoviolence and development of both individuals and communities throughout the life span.

Discussion Questions

1. Part 4 of *An Educational Resource* (pp. 77–83 in this volume and pp. 31–37 in the student version) explores the history of ethnoviolence in both the United States and the global South, addressing such issues as slavery, colonialism, and recent hate crimes and white supremacist movements. Do such historical realities influence individuals at various stages of development? If so, how?
2. In what ways does ethnoviolence obstruct the development of individuals and the development of societies? Give specific examples.
3. Some of the costs to society of ethnic conflict are listed in part 4 of *An Educational Resource* (pp. 80–81 of this volume and pp. 34–35 of the student version). On the basis of social work's person-in-environment perspective,

how is each cost relevant to particular clients and communities in the United States?

SOCIAL WORK THEORY AND PRACTICE

Objectives

1. Students will demonstrate a commitment to advocacy on behalf of exploited and oppressed ethnic communities.
2. Students will demonstrate an understanding of the need for community development approaches to solving the problem of ethnic conflict.
3. Students will increase their skills in promoting the peaceful resolution of conflicts between individuals and groups.

Discussion Questions

1. What are some ways that social workers can get involved in grassroots organizing, intervention, and advocacy in ethnic communities?
2. How can social workers help to prevent an anti-immigration backlash in their agencies and the communities in which they practice?
3. Which intervention strategies can social workers use to reduce ethnoviolence at the personal, institutional, and structural levels of society?

SOCIAL WELFARE POLICY

Objectives

1. Students will demonstrate an understanding of the connections between militarism and foreign policy and ethnic conflict.
2. Students will be able to articulate how the effects of the lack of development opportunities (for example, poverty and unemployment) and unjust development lead to ethnoviolence in the United States and the global South.
3. Students will demonstrate an awareness of how ethnoviolence impedes the social and economic development of communities and countries and the relevance of ethnic conflicts in other countries for U.S. domestic policies.
4. Students will demonstrate the ability to develop policies and programs based on

the principles of sustainable human development.

Discussion Questions

1. In part 4 of *An Educational Resource* (pp. 80–81 of this volume and pp. 34–35 of the student version), there is a discussion of how the lack of development opportunities and unjust development can lead to ethnoviolence. What are the connections between development and ethnoviolence in a specific social welfare policy?
2. There is considerable anti-immigrant sentiment in the United States today. What are some of the connections between ethnic conflict and immigration? What policies would you propose to foster a greater understanding among U.S. citizens and immigrants?

RESEARCH

Objectives

1. Students will be able to identify perspectives and biases based on race and ethnicity that underlie the presentation of social and scientific data.
2. Students will understand the effects of bias in research that are the result of racism and other forms of structural–cultural oppression.

Discussion Questions

1. In part 4 of *An Educational Resource* (p. 80 of this volume and p. 34 of the student version), it is asserted that the lack of development opportunities leads to ethnoviolence. What research evidence is there to support this claim? How would you find what the research shows?
2. Compare the social welfare and poverty indicators and statistics for different racial and ethnic groups in the United States. What do the results indicate about the connection between ethnicity and development?

FIELD PRACTICUM

Objectives

1. Students will develop skills to implement ethnically sensitive social work practice with

diverse and oppressed populations within a social justice perspective.

2. Students will develop skills in integrating and applying knowledge and theory related to diverse populations that they acquired in academic courses to actual social work situations.

3. Students will develop conflict-resolution skills with individuals, families, groups, and organizations.

Discussion Questions

1. Does ethnoviolence affect clients in your field placement? If so, how? What connections do you see between ethnoviolence and the lack of development opportunities?

2. What roles can social workers play in reducing ethnoviolence at both the macro- and microlevels?

Exercise 1—Case Studies and Short Lecture
Three Types of Hate Crimes

Purpose

To increase awareness of the different motivations of hate offenders and the need to tailor intervention strategies.

Learning Activity

Have the class read the descriptions and case examples of three types of hate crimes in *An Educational Resource* (p. 78 of this volume and p. 32 of the student version), give the short lecture, and then discuss the questions that follow.

Lecture: Study Reveals that Hate Crimes Vary Significantly by the Motivation of Offenders

A 1995 book by J. Levin and J. McDevitt, two nationally recognized authorities on hate crimes (cited in "Landmark Study Reveals," 1995), reported the results of a study that found that there were three distinct types of motivations for hate crimes.

THRILL HATE CRIMES

Levin and McDevitt found that the most common type of hate crime (58 percent) in Boston is physical assault committed by groups of offenders simply for thrills or excitement. Of these thrill hate crimes, 53 percent were committed by two or more offenders looking for trouble in the victim's neighborhood. The offenders were predominately white male teenagers, the vast majority of whom (91 percent) did not know the person they were attacking.

A particularly disturbing finding was the extent of the violence associated with thrill hate crimes. Although people often describe these incidents as "just kids causing trouble," the study indicated that 70 percent of the thrill crimes consisted of assaults. This finding directly contradicts the notion that most hate crimes are merely childish pranks and reveals that when young people gather to "hassle" someone who is African American or gay, for example, they are likely to beat, rather than to berate, their victim. The study also revealed that a wide variety of groups (including African Americans, whites, gay men and lesbians, Latinos, Asian Americans, and Jews) were targeted for violence simply to provide a few "kicks" for a group of offenders. In Boston, the most likely victims of thrill hate crimes are Latinos and Asian Americans, followed by gay men and lesbians and then African Americans; white people are the least likely to be attacked.

In thrill hate crimes, the victims are often interchangeable. Some offenders substitute one victim for another when their first choice for attack is unavailable. One member of a disfavored group can easily replace another. Furthermore, because of the growing "culture of hate," hate has become "hip" and intolerance is "in" for many people. Random hate attacks reflect the increasing social acceptability of violence and group stereotyping.

DEFENSIVE HATE CRIMES

Defensive hate crimes occur in response to other incidents that the offenders perceive as intrusion by outsiders. The offenders have a stronger commitment to prejudice than do their thrill-offender counterparts. These crimes generally involve a series of attacks perpetrated by white men, often acting alone. In this type of attack, the offender is trying to send a specific message that his victim does not belong in a particular community, school, or workplace and that anyone in the victim's group who dares "intrude" could be next.

In Levin and McDevitt's study, most of the defensive hate crimes were assaults (64 percent); only 14 percent were acts of vandalism. As with thrill hate crimes, most defensive hate crimes involved white offenders (65 percent) who did not know their victims (79 percent). In contrast to thrill hate crimes, which were usually committed by a group of attackers, the majority of defensive hate crimes were committed by individuals (61 percent).

As with thrill hate crimes in Boston, Asian Americans were the most likely group to be victimized in defensive hate crimes. Other groups— gay men and lesbians, African Americans, and Latinos—had roughly the same rate of victimization. And again, white people were the group least likely to be victimized.

MISSION HATE CRIMES

This is the most serious but the rarest type of hate crime. The offender has fully committed himself to prejudice and has allowed bigotry to take over his life. Frequently, he has joined a local chapter of the Ku Klux Klan or neo-Nazi or Skinhead group to be closer to those who espouse similar beliefs. This type of offender usually has failed to fit into society and blames his personal failures on the members of any group he believes to be different. His mission is more than to target a particular victim; it is to rid the world of all members of the "inferior" group, as well as its symbols. Although mission crimes are far less common than the other forms of hate crimes, they are associated with the most extreme violence. The bombing of the U.S. Federal Building in Oklahoma City in April 1995 was probably the quintessential mission hate crime, perpetrated by individuals whose lives are consumed with hatred not only for the federal government but possibly for African Americans and Jews as well.

TAILORING THE RESPONSE

Levin and McDevitt ("Landmark study reveals," 1995) argued that by recognizing the different kinds of hate crimes and developing policies to deal with each type, the police and other public officials should be better able to identify criminal expressions of hate and deal with the offenders effectively.

Properly distinguishing between the different types of hate crimes should also help identify the offenders. For example, a person who commits a defensive hate crime usually lives in the same neighborhood or on the same college campus as the victim, whereas a group of youths who commit a thrill hate crime usually do not live in the area where the crime is committed and are strangers to the victim.

The courts could also use information on the types of hate crimes in their sentencing procedures. For example, persons who commit defensive hate crimes are more likely to repeat their actions, so that the victims (members of a particular group) "get the message." Their underlying motivation may be complicated by in-group– out-group issues and economic issues (fear of economic insecurity owing to affirmative action, for instance). On the other hand, courts may find that those who commit thrill hate crimes, who are less likely to repeat their actions, are more suitable for alternative rehabilitation and educational programs.

DYNAMICS OF YOUTH, HATE, AND VIOLENCE

As the country grows more divided along racial and ethnic lines, the problem of youth violence is increasing. Although they constitute less than one-third of the population, youths under age 21 constitute half the perpetrators of hate crimes. Schools and colleges are often fertile ground for hate crimes. A study conducted in 1992 ("Landmark Study Reveals," 1995) reported that 25 percent of minority college students at predominantly white colleges were victims of prejudicial acts ranging from name calling and property damage "to threats and assaults." A 1990 Harris poll of high school students showed that more than half had witnessed racial confrontations at least once in a while and that half said they either approved of such incidents or would actually participate.

Discussion Questions

1. What are the differences between the three types of hate crimes? What are the similarities?
2. Should the response of the police and other authorities vary by the type of hate crime? If so, how? Be specific.
3. What social work interventions may stop the cycle of violence illustrated in each case example in part 4 of *An Educational Resource* (pp. 81–82 of this volume and pp. 35–36 of the student version)?
4. What international connections are involved in the case studies?

Exercise 2—Case Study of a Conflict Situation and the Conflict-Resolution Process

Learning Objective

To help students analyze an ethnic-conflict situation and propose alternative nonviolent resolution strategies.

Learning Activity

Have each student present a case study of a conflict situation and its conflict-resolution process, including proposed strategies for resolution that were not used in the situation. It is strongly recommended that students use experiences from their field placements for this assignment. However, a range of other conflict situations may also be used, including those from experiences in a classroom or personal experiences or ethnic conflict within a country or between two countries. Whatever situation is used should involve *ethnicity* as it is defined in part 4 of *An Educational Resource* (p. 77 of this volume and p. 31 of the student version): a people united by culture, religion, language, dialect, geographic origin, traditions, values, and symbols. The conflict may be

- intrapersonal, for example, a person (perhaps a client) who is experiencing intrapsychic conflict related to multiple racial, cultural, religious identities
- interpersonal, such as between a client and a social worker, two social workers, or members of an intimate couple
- intergroup, for instance, conflicts with societal institutions that involve ethnic differences, community ethnic groups in conflict, conflict in school between students of two diverse groups
- international, such as ethnic conflicts in the former Yugoslavia, Somalia, and other regions of the world.

The presentation should include
1. a brief definition of the conflict with a description of how the conflict started
2. an analysis of the conflict in terms of the relationship of the parties involved, strategies used by the participants, and the outcome of attempts to manage the conflict
3. the student's suggested strategies for directing the conflict toward a constructive resolution.

Source: This assignment was adapted from an assignment developed by Dr. Tiong Tan for the course "Conflict Resolution and the Helping Professions," taught at St. Thomas University, St. Paul, MN (Van Soest, 1992, p. 71).

Exercise 3—Short Lecture and Quiz on Immigration

Myths and Facts

Purpose

To increase students' knowledge about immigrants and refugees in the United States and to stimulate interest in learning more.

Learning Activity

During a time when anti-immigrant sentiment and related hate crimes are increasing, it is important for social workers to understand the facts about immigration to counteract the prejudice of individuals and institutions. Give the short lecture, then have students complete the following quiz, and follow it with a classroom discussion.

Short Lecture

There are over 100 million immigrants and refugees in the world today. This unprecedented number has prompted widespread concern about the causes and consequences of international migration.

The United States receives less than 1 percent of the world's immigrants annually. Nevertheless, it has responded to the international crisis in migration by cracking down on undocumented immigrants, tightening border controls, restricting access to political asylum, and threatening immigrants' access to public assistance programs. Most policymakers are quick to pander to racist and xenophobic fears and claims that immigration has become a primary source of this country's economic instability. However, dramatic political and economic changes since the 1980s have produced new migrant populations and patterns that defy "traditional" immigration controls. The root causes of international migration are often intertwined and include economic, political (most of today's refugees are fleeing conditions of violence from conflicts in their countries of origin), environmental (millions are being displaced because the land they live on has become toxic or is unable to support them, primarily because of national and multinational business ventures), and ethnic tensions unleashed by national instabilities and conflicts and fomented by political adversaries.

The dominant flow of refugees is from the global South to the global North—a manifestation of uneven social, political, and economic development and conflict that require cooperation and collective action among countries and regions. Social workers, who often work directly with immigrants, should make their voices heard in the policymaking arena, speaking out against simplistic responses and heightening awareness of ignorance, racial intolerance, and xenophobia.

Discussion Questions

1. What did you learn from the exercise?
2. What are the implications of some of the facts for social policy related to the U.S. economic system? educational system? health care system? judicial system?

1. Since 1990, the poorest immigrants to the United States have come from
   a. Africa
   b. Asia
   c. Central America
   d. the former Soviet Union

2. The continent from which the highest percentage of immigrants to the United States are high school graduates is
   a. Europe
   b. Central America
   c. Africa
   d. Asia

3. The immigrant population that earns the highest median household income in the United States is
   a. Mexican
   b. English
   c. Indian
   d. African

4. In 1910, 15 percent of the U.S. population was foreign born. In 1990, the percentage of the population who were foreign born was
   a. 8 percent
   b. 10 percent
   c. 18 percent
   d. 22 percent

5. Studies by the Urban Institute found that for every 100 new immigrants
   a. employment decreases by 62 jobs
   b. the number of jobs stays the same
   c. employment increases by 46 jobs
   d. it is impossible to tell how the job market will react

6. A study of Los Angeles County showed that the county spent $2.45 billion in 1991–92 on schools and other services for resident immigrants. In that same period, resident immigrants
   a. paid no taxes
   b. paid $1.7 billion in taxes
   c. paid $4.3 billion in taxes
   d. the amount of taxes paid is impossible to calculate

7. Nationally, immigrants receive about $5 billion annually in welfare benefits. Approximately how much do they earn and pay in taxes?
   a. They earn $10 billion and pay $1.3 billion in taxes.
   b. They earn $15 billion and pay $3 billion in taxes.
   c. They earn $100 billion and pay $15 billion in taxes.
   d. They earn $240 billion and pay $85 billion in taxes.

8. Increased immigration tends to
   a. produce higher wages for immigrants
   b. produce higher wages for U.S. citizens
   c. produce lower wages for immigrants
   d. produce lower wages for U.S. citizens

9. A 1992 survey found that it is common for Americans to go to Mexico for health care: Over 90 percent of the Mexican physicians who were surveyed had treated Americans. The major reason why U.S. citizens go to Mexico for treatment is that
   a. they believe that Mexican physicians are more highly qualified
   b. Mexican physicians accept all types of health insurance
   c. Mexican physicians and prescription drugs are cheaper
   d. the climate is better

10. In northern California, an undocumented person who is seeking political or economic asylum may be jailed and
    a. not be accused of a crime: true or false?
    b. allowed bail: true or false?
    c. allowed to be represented by a public defender: true or false?
    d. not allowed to have a trial by jury: true or false?
    e. may be placed in a maximum security facility: true or false?
    f. if a woman, may be locked down for up to 22 hours a day: true or false?

1. **d.** Recent immigrants from the former Soviet Union are among the poorest and the least employed, far more so than Latin American or Asian newcomers, according to the U.S. Bureau of the Census ("Census Data Reveal," 1993).

2. **c.** Almost 88 percent of African immigrants had a high school diploma and 47 percent had a bachelor's degree or better, according to a study by the U.S Bureau of the Census ("African Immigrants Best Educated," 1993). Africans as a group are also better educated than the general U.S. population: Only 77 percent of U.S.-born adults have a high school diploma and just over 20 percent have a bachelor's degree or higher.

3. **b.** The median household income for an immigrant from the United Kingdom was $41,158, and for a Japanese immigrant, $35,487. The median household incomes of most Central American and African immigrants were in the high teens; of Mexicans, $16,712; and of Indians, $22,231. The lowest paid are Vietnamese ($12,507), Laotians ($11,750), and those from the former Soviet Union ($8,248) ("America's Diverse Immigrants," 1993). A question to ponder is this: If Africans as a group are the most highly educated, why is their median household income ($17,871) in the lower half of the income scale?

4. **a.** The figure of 8 percent is from Susan Lapham, a demographer at the U.S. Bureau of the Census, who reported the bureau's study on immigrants (see "Census Data Reveal," 1993).

5. **c.** For these studies, see "From Bill to Pete" (1993) in the reference list, p. 75.

6. **c.** For more on this study, see "From Bill to Pete" (1993) in the reference list, p. 75.

7. **d.** For a report of these figures, see "Immigrants" (1992) in the reference list, p. 75.

8. **c.** Although wages fell in California during the wave of immigration in the mid-1980s, immigrants absorbed most of the adverse impact (see Muller & Espenshade, 1985, cited in *Advocate's Quick Guide*, 1993).

9. **c.** For a report of this survey, see "Going to Mexico" (1992), cited in *Advocate's Quick Reference Guide* (1993).

10. **a.** true, **b.** false, **c.** false, **d.** true, **e.** true, and **f.** true. For further information, see "Give Me Your Tired, Your Poor" (1993) in the reference list, p. 75.

Source: The quiz was prepared by the Applied Research Center (1322 Webster Street, #402, Oakland, CA 94612) as part of one of 15 "issue study groups" for its Campaign on Community Safety and Police Accountability. Printed with permission.

REFERENCES

Advocate's quick reference guide to immigration research. (1993, August). Washington, DC: National Council of La Raza.

African immigrants best educated in the U.S., census shows. (1993, September 23). *Contra Costa Times.*

America's diverse immigrants. (1993, September 23). *San Francisco Chronicle.*

Census data reveal wide immigrant diversity (1993, September 23). *San Francisco Examiner.*

From Bill to Pete. (1993, September). *RaceFile.*

Give me your tired, your poor: The jailing of immigrants in Alameda County. (1993, Summer). *The California Prisoner.*

Immigrants: How they're helping the economy. (1992, July 13). *Business Week.*

Landmark study reveals hate crimes vary significantly by offender motivation. (1995, August). *Klanwatch Intelligence Report,* pp. 7–9.

FOR FURTHER READING

American Friends Service Committee. (1994, July). *Operation Blockade: A city divided. A report from the Immigration Law Enforcement Monitoring Project (ILEMP).* Philadelphia: Author.

This report is about Operation Blockade, an initiative of the U.S. Border Patrol that cut the twin cities of El Paso, Texas, and Ciudad Juarez, Mexico, off from each other by positioning 400 agents and their vehicles along a 20-mile stretch of the border. It proposes immigration and border-control policies that are based on a mutual agreement between Mexico and the United States and that respect human rights and dignity.

Conflict and development. (1994). Washington, DC: Panos Institute.

This educational module examines social, economic, and political factors within and among countries, especially developing ones, that contribute to violent conflict. It also describes the impact of conflict and the ways in which armed conflict reduces the potential for sustainable human development and discusses current approaches to conflict resolution, prevention, and peacekeeping efforts.

Cozic, C. P. (Ed.). (1995). *Ethnic conflict.* San Diego, CA: Greenhaven Press.

This book presents a wide range of suggestions to alleviate the brewing conflict within and among ethnic groups in the United States. Several writers discuss how Americans should reconcile their ethnic heritages, similarities, and differences.

Journal of Multicultural Social Work. Published quarterly. Haworth Press, 10 Alice Street, Binghamton, NY 13904-1580; phone 607-722-5857.

This journal is dedicated to the examination of multicultural social issues related to social work policy, research, theory, and practice from an international perspective.

Premdas, R. (1995). *Fiji: Ethnic conflict and development.* Brookfield, VT: Ashgate Publishing.

This book examines the link between ethnic conflict and development by providing a detailed background of the evolution of the communal strife in Fiji, particularly the role of ethnic entrepreneurs and outbidders in instigating latent ethnic fears for political purposes. It argues that the introduction of democratic policies in a multiethnic state requires special institutions that do not cultivate zero-sum rivalry over control of the state and its resources. In Fiji, open ethnic competition led to the seizure of power by one ethnic group over the other. An ethnically inspired military government oversaw the infringement of basic human rights and the installation of a new apartheid regime.

Yanoov, B. Chetkow, & Korazim, Y. (Eds.). (1994, July). *Conflict resolution by social workers in Israel: A reader.* Tel-Aviv: Israel Association of Social Workers (93, Arlosorov Street, Tel-Aviv, Israel; phone 3-695-6482, fax 3-696-4308).

This book is a compilation of papers that were presented at a mini plenary session on conflict resolution at the 1994 World Conference of Social Workers in Sri Lanka. It includes some theories of conflict and the practice of conflict resolution, as well as case studies.

CHAPTER 4-2

ETHNICITY

EDUCATIONAL RESOURCE

The world is enriched by the ethnic and cultural diversity of the people who inhabit it. Yet few countries are untouched by ethnic and racial violence. Despite the United States' claim to being a true melting-pot society, the mass media are filled with accounts of intergroup conflict, hate crimes, and random acts of violence perpetrated on the basis of people's skin color, ethnicity, and religious affiliation. Meanwhile, ethnic conflict is rife in many other parts of the world, including the Middle East, Central Asia, Africa, and post-Communist Eastern Europe, sending a steady stream of immigrants to the United States and other relatively stable countries.

Ethnic violence is of particular concern to the social work profession, which has a long history of working to promote social justice for oppressed populations. By working with people from different ethnic groups, professionals in the field have developed an understanding of the complex relationships between poverty and prejudice and each group's role in interethnic conflict based on their history of domination or subordination.

Part 4 explores some of the various causes and consequences of racial and ethnic conflict around the world. It examines the link between ethnic violence in the United States and the global South and discusses how the lack of development opportunities fuels ethnic violence and how sustainable human development can help alleviate this global problem.

ETHNICITY AND ETHNOVIOLENCE DEFINED

Ethnic Groups and Ethnicity

Ethnic groups are made up of people united by any combination of the following: culture, religion, language, dialect, geographic origin, traditions, values, and symbols (Thernstrom, Orlov, & Handlin, 1980). Estimates of the number of distinct ethnic groups in the world range from 575 groups that are either current national states or have the potential to claim that status to 5,000 different ethnic groups based on distinct languages (Nielsson & Jones, 1993, cited in Gurr, 1993; Nietschmann, 1987). Pinderhughes (1989) defined ethnicity as

> connectedness based on commonalities where specific aspects of cultural patterns are shared and where transmission over time creates a common history. . . . Race, while a biological term, takes on ethnic meaning when and if members of that biological group have evolved specific ways of living. . . . Ethnic values and practices foster the survival of the group and of individuals within. (p. 6)

Ethnoviolence

Ethnoviolence refers to violence perpetrated primarily on the basis of one's ethnicity. There is no single cause of ethnic violence. Rather, it stems from multiple, interrelated factors, including the following:

- hateful revenge and territorial disputes, often based on a history of dominant and subordinate relationships between two groups
- injustice and the unequal distribution of economic resources and political power
- repression and neglect of minority populations
- competition over limited resources
- prejudice and ignorance (*Conflict and Development*, 1994; Pacific Northwest NASW Center, 1994).

TYPES OF HATE CRIMES

Thrill Hate Crimes

In thrill hate crimes, offenders target violence against individuals from another group—often Asians, Hispanics, gay men and lesbians, or African Americans—to give themselves a thrill. The victims are often interchangeable. Some offenders substitute one victim for another when their first choice for attack is unavailable, and one member of a disfavored group can easily replace another. Because of the growing "culture of hate," for many people hate has become hip and intolerance is "in." Random attacks of hate reflect the increasing social acceptability of violence and group stereotyping ("Landmark Study Reveals," 1995).

Defensive Hate Crimes

Defensive hate crimes occur in response to incidents that the perpetrators perceive as intrusion by outsiders. These perpetrators have a stronger commitment to prejudice than their counterparts who commit thrill hate crimes. Defensive hate crimes generally involve a series of attacks perpetrated by white men, often acting alone. The perpetrators are trying to send a specific message that their victims do not belong in a particular community, school, or workplace and that anyone in the victim's group who dares "intrude" could be next ("Landmark Study Reveals," 1995).

Mission Hate Crimes

Mission hate crimes are the most serious but rarest of all hate crimes. The perpetrator has fully

committed himself to prejudice and has allowed bigotry to take over his life. Frequently, he has joined a local chapter of the Ku Klux Klan or a neo-Nazi or Skinhead group to be closer to those who espouse similar beliefs. This type of perpetrator usually has failed to fit into society and blames his personal failures on the members of any group he believes to be different. His mission is more than to target a particular victim; he is seeking to rid the world of all members of the "inferior" group, as well as its symbols ("Landmark Study Reveals," 1995).

CASE STUDIES

Roxbury: A Thrill Hate Crime

One winter evening, three 22-year-old white men, bored and looking for something to do, decided to go out and "start some trouble." They picked up several bricks from a construction site and drove to Roxbury, a predominately black section of Boston. As they were driving, they saw a 42-year-old African American man walking alone near his home. The three young men drove up behind the victim and struck him with one of the bricks. Then they quickly drove out of the area and back to their homes ("Landmark Study Reveals," 1995).

San Francisco: A Defensive Hate Crime

A 32-year-old Asian American male cabdriver was driving through a neighborhood in San Francisco. When the taxi stopped at a traffic light, a 19-year-old local white man smashed a hockey stick through the cab's rear window. He warned the cabdriver to leave the area and told him that he did not belong in the United States ("Landmark Study Reveals," 1995).

Medway: A Mission Hate Crime

Four white male Skinheads from Medway, a suburb of Boston, had previously painted swastikas on public structures in and around their town, but had not been arrested for any of these incidents. The four youths began to escalate their violence until they drove to the South End of Boston one night, looking for gays to bash. They approached two white men they thought were gay and began to harass them verbally. When the victims attempted to escape, the Skinheads took baseball bats from their van and beat the men. Upon arresting the four perpetrators, two of whom had White Power tatoos on their bodies, the Boston police discovered that their van and their homes were full of hate literature ("Landmark Study Reveals," 1995).

ETHNOVIOLENCE: A GLOBAL PROBLEM

Throughout the world, ethnic conflict is rooted in relationships in which one group dominates another based on an ideology of superiority. The "superior" group seeks to preserve its power and privileges through violence or the threat of violence against those it perceives as different or inferior (McLemore, 1994). Ethnoviolence on the personal level, combined with collusion at the institutional level, functions as a kind of terrorism (Sheffield, 1995). In his autobiographical novel *Black Boy*, Wright (1937) noted: "The things that influenced my conduct as a Negro did not have to happen to me directly: I needed but to hear of them to feel their full effects in the deepest layers of my consciousness. Indeed the white brutality that I had not seen was a more effective control of my behavior than that which I knew" (p. 65).

History of Violence

In the United States, white people became the dominant group through exploitation and force, beginning with violence committed against indigenous people by white European settlers in the 1600s. For decades, the government and its agents often institutionally organized and sanctioned hate violence. State violence was committed not only against Native Americans but also captured and enslaved Africans, free African Americans, and other racial groups (Weiss, 1990).

Violence based on hate has been both spontaneous and organized in the United States. Established hate groups have played an integral role in perpetuating an environment of fear for Americans from diverse racial and ethnic groups (Sheffield, 1995). The Ku Klux Klan, one of the better-known organized hate groups, has been responsible for some of the most brutal violence in American history. Between 1889 and 1941, the Klan lynched 3,811 African Americans in this country (Sheffield, 1995).

In recent years, hate crimes have been on the rise in the United States. Klan members have developed ties with a number of other hate groups, such as Holocaust denial groups, the neo-Nazi Skinhead movement, and the Aryan Nation. The movement as a whole has become more sophisticated in its organizing techniques. A survey of state and municipal law enforcement agencies reported a 19.3 percent rise in bias crimes during 1992 (*White Supremacy in the 90s*, 1994). In the early to mid-1990s, only 25,000 Americans were hard-core activists for the white supremacist movement, but approximately 200,000 people subscribed to racist publications, attended marches and rallies, and donated money to the cause. In addition, as of 1994, 150 independent racist radio and TV shows aired weekly, reaching millions of sympathizers (*White Supremacy in the 90s*, 1994).

Like the United States, the global South has a history of hate violence. In many countries, colonizing powers played a key role in igniting ethnic tensions that still exist. In Africa, for example, from the mid-15th to the mid-20th century, colonizing powers redrew national boundaries, usually ignoring well-established tribal cultural patterns. People were counted and classified in discrete and bounded groups; thus, new categories of identity were created to replace the overlapping and multiple cultural identities that had existed before. Furthermore, colonial state policies promoted differential treatment of ethnic groups, which led to extensive economic and social disparities. After independence, systems of inequity continued, fueling ethnic conflicts (Jalali & Lipset, 1993).

The violence goes on. Around the globe, ethnoviolence has reached alarming proportions. Most civil wars in the post–Cold War world have been ethnic, tribal, or religious in nature. From Serbs practicing "ethnic cleansing" of Muslims to Indonesian troops firing on unarmed protesters in

East Timor to police brutality in Los Angeles, hate violence is a global problem (Shuman & Harvey, 1993). As of 1992, 29 wars between ethnic groups raged worldwide. From these conflicts, 3,351,000 people, mostly civilians, died (Sivard, 1993).

ETHNOVIOLENCE AND DEVELOPMENT: MAKING THE CONNECTION

Militarism fuels ethnoviolence and impedes development. Although the causes of ethnic conflict are usually domestic or regional disputes, these disputes often escalate into armed confrontation when wealthier nations provide weapons or the financial means to purchase them (Deng & Zartman, 1991, cited in *Conflict and Development*, 1994). During the Cold War, both the United States and the Soviet Union provided military assistance to opposite sides in conflicts in the global South. These superpowers had a hand in driving violent ethnic conflicts in Sudan, Somalia, Angola, and Guatemala, for example. In the 1990s, the United States continues to be one of the top producers of weapons, and nations of the global South are major purchasers (Hartung, 1994).

In some countries, governments and armed forces have inflamed historic ethnic and religious tensions to consolidate their power and elite status. In Rwanda, for example, tensions between the Hutu and Tutsi ethnic groups have been systematically heightened by different rulers throughout history. German and Belgian colonial powers favored the Tutsis for their lighter skin and greater height. At independence in 1962, violence took the lives of 100,000 to 200,000 people. The ensuing years saw an ongoing struggle for control between the Tutsis and the Hutus. When a plane crash killed the Hutu presidents of Rwanda and Burundi in April 1994, the accident touched off a wave of ethnically based killings that left 500,000 dead. Subsequently, more than 1 million people fled to Zaire in one week in July 1994. Decades of development achievements have been destroyed (*Conflict and Development*, 1994; *Hunger 1995*, 1995).

Ethnoviolence obstructs development. Ethnic conflict generates multiple costs to society.

Among them are the
- denial of fundamental human rights and freedoms
- breakdown of political order
- displacement of thousands of people, mainly women and children, who are forced to flee their homes
- depletion of environmental resources, reducing the land's ability to produce crops and sustain people
- destruction of roads, bridges, food supplies, and other basic aspects of the infrastructure
- interruption of economic development and individuals' efforts to provide for themselves and their families (*Conflict and Development*, 1994).

Sudan is one country where interethnic war has had a devastating effect on human and societal development. In 1984, after years of state-sanctioned religious and economic oppression, the people in the southern half of Sudan (composed mostly of Christians and tribal groups) launched a guerrilla war against the Muslim-dominated northern half of the country, the home of the national government. Largely a subsistence-agriculture society in which people survive on the food they grow, Sudan was thrown into famine when war broke out and people were unable to plant or harvest their crops. More than 500,000 people had died in the conflict by 1994. Advances in development, such as schools, health clinics, and agricultural research programs, were destroyed throughout the country (*Conflict and Development*, 1994; *Hunger 1995*, 1995).

The lack of development opportunities leads to ethnoviolence. The UN Development Programme (1994) cited the lack of income security as one of the main root causes of ethnic violence in many countries. The fact that only one-quarter of the world's people are assured a basic, steady income helps explain why the planet is rife with competitive, ethnic conflict.

Social and economic inequity often correlate with racial and ethnic origin, constituting what can be called passive ethnoviolence (Dasgupta, 1968). Consider these statistics:
- In the United States, the unemployment rate for African Americans is twice that of white people (DiNitto, 1995).

- Poverty rates among African Americans and Hispanic Americans are nearly three times those of white people (UN Development Programme, 1994; Weiss, 1990).
- During South Africa's apartheid regime, if white South Africa had been a separate country, it would have ranked 24th in the world in human development, and black South Africa would have placed 123rd (*Hunger 1995*, 1995).
- In Guatemala, where Mayan Indians make up the majority of the population, the life expectancy for Mayan men is 48 compared to 65 for non-Mayan men (*Hunger 1995*, 1995).

Unjust development can lead to ethnoviolence. "Progress" itself can be a source of conflict when it serves the interests of wealthier people and excludes traditionally marginalized groups. For example, indigenous people around the world have had their traditional lands and resources usurped and exploited by vast logging, mining, and petroleum operations in the name of economic development. Their calls for justice have often been violently suppressed. In Nigeria, for instance, the extraction of petroleum from the lands of the Ogoni people has made the country among the richest in Africa, while the Ogoni continue to suffer from extreme poverty (*Conflict and Development*, 1994).

Unjust development takes other forms as well. Hoff and Polack (1993) pointed out that to meet international demands for the repayment of debts, governments of countries in the global South often force peasants to abandon their traditional, often environmentally sound, farming practices or to abandon their land altogether to produce cash crops for export. The results: the disruption of traditional ways of life, the destruction of local ecosystems, hunger, deprivation, indignity—all of which are forms of violence. Such conditions ultimately give rise to political instability and physical violence.

SUSTAINABLE HUMAN DEVELOPMENT: AN ANTIDOTE TO ETHNOVIOLENCE

As Rigoberto Menchú, of Guatemala, who received the Nobel Prize for Peace in 1992, stated:

> It is not that peace is merely the absence of war, combat or conflict; rather, it is the absence of the conditions that give rise to war: intolerance, disrespect, arrogance, rigidity—and most of all, indignity and hunger. When people's needs and desires are satisfied, we can begin to talk about building peace. (Quoted in Oxfam America, 1992)

The basic premise of part 4 is that real solutions to ethnic violence lie in promoting sustainable human development. For the world to be a place where all people can live in safety, dignity, peace, and economic security, the following actions are needed:

- Encourage the redistribution of land, resources, and income to reduce the gap between the wealthy elite and the vast impoverished underclass.
- Promote strong, participatory democracies, in which people are given ample opportunities to be involved in decisions that affect their lives.
- Promote vibrant civil societies.
- Provide constitutional protections for racial and ethnic groups, which make a pluralistic society possible. The U.S. Supreme Court's enforcement of the Fourteenth Amendment to the Constitution ensures legal protection for American racial and ethnic groups. As a result, most civil rights movements in the United States have fought for pluralism and fairness, rather than for secession and separatism.
- Help nations become self-sufficient in the provision of such basic needs as food, safe water, shelter, clothing, and health care.
- Foster greater understanding among racial and ethnic groups and promote the peaceful resolution of conflicts (Shuman & Harvey, 1993).

Strong democratic systems and sustainable human development can go a long way toward eliminating sources of conflict. Nonetheless, some groups and nations will inevitably have disagreements with other groups and nations. When conflicts do occur, every attempt should be made to resolve them through nonviolent means.

Ethnic tensions can be reduced through programs that foster a greater understanding of the different cultures and life experiences of various ethnic groups. When possible, ethnic groups should be encouraged to discuss their historic differences and to forgive each other for past mistakes.

CIVIL SOCIETY: GIVING POWER TO THE PEOPLE

Civil society is the web of nongovernmental organizations and movements that empower citizens to take action and solve problems on their own behalf. Such organizations serve as a critical mechanism for creating new solutions to social, economic, and political problems at the grassroots level and for defusing potentially explosive situations that are fueled by governmental inaction.

In the United States, groups, such as the United Way, the National Association for the Advancement of Colored People, and labor unions, have played a key role in fighting racial injustice and seeking fair treatment and better working conditions for all citizens.

The videotape *Not in Our Town* (1995) tells the inspiring story of how Billings, Montana, took action against a wave of violent hate crimes that swept the community. The local painters union repainted the home of a Native American woman after it was spray painted with racist graffiti. The human rights coalition organized more than 100 community members to collect more than 6,000 signatures of support. After someone threw a cinderblock through the window of a Jewish child's bedroom because a menorah was displayed in the window, the local newspaper published a colorful full-page photograph of a menorah and asked people throughout Billings to put it in their window as an act of solidarity. More than 10,000 photographs were displayed. The rash of hate crimes stopped.

Elsewhere in the world, nongovernmental organizations are breaking new ground in fostering ethnic harmony. For example, the Neve Shalom Kibbutz, located between Jerusalem and Tel Aviv, has established the only Jewish–Arab bilingual school system in the country to promote the ideals of peaceful coexistence and equality between the two groups (American Friends of Neve Shalom, 1996).

WHAT YOU CAN DO

- Find out how you can become involved in the UN's International Decade of the World's Indigenous People, launched in December 1994. Contact Julian Burger, Centre for Human Rights (Palais des Nations, CH-1211 Geneva 10, Switzerland; phone 41-22-917-3413, fax 41-22-917-0212).
- Help prevent an anti-immigration backlash by initiating community-based educational activities, such as cultural awareness days.
- Get involved in grassroots organizing, intervention, and advocacy in ethnic communities.
- Advocate for strong democracies that include and involve all ethnic groups, both at home and overseas.
- Promote peace and social justice in all practice settings through the use of nonviolent conflict-resolution strategies.
- Work to reduce violence and ethnic stereotyping in the mass media.

REFERENCES

American Friends of Neve Shalom/Wahat Al-Salam. (1996). (Brochure available from the organization at 121 Sixth Avenue, Suite 502, New York, NY 10013; phone 212-226-9246)

Conflict and development. (1994). Washington, DC: Panos Institute.

Dasgupta, S. (1968). Gandhian concept of nonviolence and its relevance today to professional social work. *Indian Journal of Social Work, 29,* 113–122.

DiNitto, D. (1995). *Social welfare politics and public policy* (4th ed.). Boston: Allyn & Bacon.

Gurr, T. R. (1993). *Minorities at risk: A global view of ethnopolitical conflicts.* Washington, DC: U.S. Institute of Peace.

Hartung, W. D. (1994). *And weapons for all.* New York: HarperCollins.

Hoff, M. D., & Polack, R. J. (1993). Social dimensions of the environmental crisis: Challenges for social work. *Social Work, 38,* 204–211.

Hunger 1995: Causes of hunger. (1995). (Available from Bread for the World Institute, 1100 Wayne Avenue South, Suite 1000, Silver Spring, MD 20910; phone 301-608-2400)

Jalali, R., & Lipset, S. M. (1993). Racial and ethnic conflicts: A global perspective. In D. Caraley (Ed.), *New world politics: Power, ethnicity, and democracy* (pp. 55–76). Montpelier, VT: Capital City Press.

Landmark study reveals hate crimes vary significantly by offender motivation. (1995, August). *Klanwatch Intelligence Report* (Montgomery, AL), pp. 7–9.

McLemore, S. D. (1994). *Racial and ethnic relations in America*. Boston: Allyn & Bacon.

Nietschmann, B. (1987). The third world war. *Cultural Survival Quarterly, 11*(3), 1–6.

Not in Our Town [videotape]. (1995). (Available from We Do the Work, 5867 Ocean View Drive, Oakland, CA 94618; phone 510-547-8484)

Oxfam America. (1992). [Campaign materials for the Fast for a World Harvest]. (available from Oxfam America, 26 West Street, Boston, MA 02111; phone 617-482-1211)

Pacific Northwest NASW Center on Violence, Development, and Ethnicity (Idaho, Oregon, and Washington NASW chapters). (1994). *Research brief* (Summary report submitted to the Violence and Development Project). Portland, OR: Author.

Pinderhughes, E. (1989). *Understanding race, ethnicity and power*. New York: Free Press.

Sheffield, C. (1995). Hate-violence. In P. S. Rothenberg (Ed.), *Race, class and gender in the United States: An integrated study* (pp. 432–441). New York: St. Martin's Press.

Shuman, M., & Harvey, H. (1993). *Security without war: A post–Cold War foreign policy*. Boulder, CO: Westview Press.

Sivard, R. L. (1993). *World military and social expenditures 1993*. Washington, DC: World Priorities.

Thernstrom, S., Orlov, A., & Handlin, O. (Eds.). (1980). *Harvard encyclopedia of American ethnic groups*. Cambridge, MA: Belknap Press.

United Nations Development Programme. (1994). *Human development report, 1994*. New York: Oxford University Press.

Weiss, J. C. (1990). Violence motivated by bigotry: Ethnoviolence. In L. Ginsberg et al. (Eds.), *Encyclopedia of social work, 18th edition, 1990 supplement* (pp. 307–319). Silver Spring, MD: NASW Press.

White supremacy in the 90s. (1994). (Available from the Center for Democratic Renewal, PO Box 50469, Atlanta, GA 30302; phone 404-221-0025)

Wright, R. (1937). *Black boy*. New York: Harper & Bros.

ADDITIONAL RESOURCES

Center for Democratic Renewal
PO Box 50469
Atlanta, GA 30302-0469
Phone: 404-221-0025

A national clearinghouse for information about the white supremacist movement in the United States.

Center on Rights Development
Graduate School of International Studies
University of Denver
Denver, CO 80208
Phone: 303-871-2523 or 303-871-2313

An international human rights program that focuses on Africa and indigenous peoples' movements.

Panos Institute
1025 T. Jefferson St., Suite 105
Washington, DC 20007
Phone: 202-965-5177

A research institute that publishes educational materials about the development process, including social conflict.

U.S. Committee for Refugees
1717 Massachusetts Avenue, NW, Suite 701
Washington, DC 20036
Phone: 202-347-3507

An organization that documents conditions of refugees, asylum seekers, and persons who have been displaced by violence or persecution. Presses for humane treatment and the protection of human rights.

PART 5

DRUG ABUSE
ENDING THE GLOBAL EPIDEMIC

CHAPTER 5-1

DRUG ABUSE

CURRICULUM

Part 5 focuses on the drug abuse–violence–maldevelopment complex of problems. It discusses the negative effects of the production, trafficking, and abuse of illegal drugs on individuals, families, and communities throughout the world; the role of social work in helping to solve these interconnected problems; and implications for social policies. Case studies illustrate the effects of drug abuse on individuals and communities.

GENERAL OBJECTIVES

1. Students will be able to describe parallel conditions of violence in the United States and in less economically advantaged nations.
2. Students will demonstrate a broadened understanding of violence and the role of the social work profession in solving the problem on a global scale.
3. Students will demonstrate an increased interest in learning from successful interventions by human services workers in the global South and in the United States.
4. Students will be able to define key concepts, such as sustainable human development, global North, and global South.
5. Students will demonstrate an awareness of social work's commitment to social justice by describing how violence and oppression affect vulnerable populations worldwide.

The objectives and discussion questions in the following section are presented by curriculum area. The questions may be used for classroom discussion or in written assignments. They are based on part 5 of *An Educational Resource* (pp. 95–102 in this volume and pp. 39–46 in the student version).

HUMAN BEHAVIOR IN THE SOCIAL ENVIRONMENT

Objectives

1. Students will demonstrate a basic understanding of the interrelated factors that contribute to the production, use, and abuse of illegal drugs, especially cocaine and crack cocaine, and addiction to them on a global scale.
2. Students will demonstrate an understanding of the deleterious effects of the abuse of illegal drugs and violence on the biopsychosocial development of people at various levels of human systems throughout the world.

Discussion Questions

1. What negative and positive effects does the production of illegal drugs, such as cocaine, have on the development of individuals, families, and communities in the global South?
2. In part 5 of *An Educational Resource* (pp. 95–96 in this volume and pp. 39–40 in the student version), drug trafficking is briefly discussed. What are the different levels of trafficking? What are some of the effects of trafficking at different levels on the development of both individual and societal systems?
3. What is the impact of drug consumption on the development of individuals, communities, and entire societies?

SOCIAL WORK THEORY AND PRACTICE

Objectives

1. Students will be able to develop a practice model that addresses the multiple goals of effective interventions in the drug abuse–violence–maldevelopment complex.
2. Students will be able to describe how the model they develop is ethically sound, knowledgeably grounded, and practical.

Discussion Questions

1. Part 5 of *An Educational Resource* (pp. 96–98 in this volume and pp. 40–42 in the student version) discusses the production, trafficking, and consumption of drugs and how each is related to issues of violence and development. What are the implications of that discussion for social work interventions?
2. What roles can social work play in reducing the production of drugs? In reducing drug trafficking? In reducing drug consumption? In helping to prevent future production, trafficking, and consumption?

SOCIAL WELFARE POLICY

Objectives

1. Students will demonstrate the ability to examine and critique selected cross-national approaches that address various links among drug abuse, violence, and maldevelopment and to assess the effectiveness of these approaches in the prevention, remediation, treatment, or rehabilitation of drug abuse.
2. Students will demonstrate the ability to conduct a comparative analysis of two or more policies, programs, and services and to explain which approach is the most comprehensive in addressing the drug abuse–violence–maldevelopment complex.

Discussion Questions

1. What impacts do current domestic and international development policies and programs have on the production, trafficking, and consumption of illegal drugs?

2. Part 5 of *An Educational Resource* (pp. 100–101 in this volume and pp. 44–45 in the student version) presents sustainable human (socioeconomic or social) development as a way to curtail drug-related violence. What changes in domestic and foreign policies are needed to promote sustainable human development in such a way as to reduce the production, trafficking, and consumption of illegal drugs?

RESEARCH

Objectives

1. Students will be able to identify sources of research data related to the production, distribution, and consumption of illegal drugs on a global scale.
2. Students will demonstrate an ability to frame critical research questions aimed at exploring connections among the production, distribution, and use of illegal drugs; socioeconomic development; and violence.

Discussion Questions

1. What kinds of research can social workers do to find the most efficient ways to help people cope with the drug abuse–violence–maldevelopment complex of problems?
2. What topical or substantive areas of research are needed the most with regard to the complex of problems in your community?

FIELD PRACTICUM

Objectives

1. Students will demonstrate a broadened understanding of the role of the social work profession in helping to solve the interconnected problems of drug abuse, violence, and maldevelopment on a local, regional, or global scale.
2. Students will demonstrate the ability to apply knowledge regarding drug abuse, violence, and maldevelopment to a particular client or agency, community, society, or world situation and to evaluate critically the effectiveness of the application.

Discussion Questions

1. What is the relevance of the discussion in part 5 of *An Educational Resource* (pp. 96–98 in this volume and pp. 40–42 in the student version) on the production, distribution, and consumption of illegal drugs for your field placement? What global connections does the discussion help you make?
2. What strategies to achieve sustainable human development are needed to address all three levels of the drug problem—production, distribution, and consumption—related to clients with whom you work?

ASSESSMENT OF CASE STUDIES

CASE STUDY 1
Weasel and the Logan 30

Ask the students to read the case study of Weasel and his drug deals in part 5 of *An Educational Resource* (p. 98 in this volume and p. 42 in the student version). Then guide them in assessing the problems with the following questions.

Discussion Questions

You are a new social worker in a community-based neighborhood agency on Logan Avenue that provides social services. Among other things, your job is to assess problems in the community and propose a course of action. Develop a plan to address the complex consequences of high drug trafficking in the neighborhood described in the case study.

The following questions can assist you in developing a preliminary assessment of this neighborhood's complex problems:

1. What are the major social problems in this neighborhood? Identify and list them.
2. Who is the victim, and why?
3. Whom would you target for intervention (individuals, families, neighborhood or community groups, or national or international bodies)?
4. What are the main problems the target group faces?
5. What strategies of intervention would you propose to reduce or resolve the target group's problems?

6. How would you handle differences in values or in cultural orientation that you may encounter in the community?
7. How will you face your own issues?

CASE STUDY 2
Julie

Ask the students to read the case study of Julie in part 5 of *An Educational Resource* (pp. 98–99 in this volume and pp. 42–43 in the student version). Then use the following questions to stimulate discussion.

Discussion Questions

1. What impact does Julie's use of cocaine have on her personal development?
2. Julie raises several issues concerning the use of illegal drugs: personal and cultural freedom, moral assumptions, and the policy on legal and illicit drugs. How are these issues related to drug abuse, violence, and maldevelopment?
3. Do occasional users of illegal drugs such as Julie contribute to maldevelopment and violence through their drug use? If so, at what level? If not, why?
4. Suppose you are a social work outreach worker. What strategies would you use to reach drug users such as Julie? If Julie does not view her own drug use as a problem, should you as a social worker see it as one? Why or why not? Is Julie considered to be a user, an abuser, or an addict?
5. What is your value base for determining whether Julie is a user, an abuser, or an addict?
6. Do you think that contradictory values (held by Julie, society, or the government) are a problem in the case study?
7. Do powerful corporate and government interests have an impact on national and international drug policies? If so, how? If not, why?
8. What can social workers do to change national and international drug policies? Be specific.

Exercise 1—Role-Playing and Discussion
Three Vignettes

The following three vignettes, supplied by the Midwest NASW Center on Violence,

Development, and Substance Abuse (Illinois, Indiana, Michigan, and Ohio chapters), may be copied for classroom use. Ask the students to enact the vignettes as role plays and then use the questions for discussion.

Vignette 1: Peru

Fortino drives his jeep up the muddy road that cuts through the verdant valley. It is a trip that he and his family members have been making for many generations. Fortino is on his way to the fields he tends, where he and his family will harvest this season's crop. Unlike the harvests he made with his father, his crop is not coffee. The crop that he now farms is coca. Fortino knows that his crop will eventually end up in the United States as crack, but he does not view his involvement in the cocaine industry as a problem. He and members of his family have been chewing coca a long time, and so did his ancestors. The mild buzz gained from this practice helps him and other farmers work for extended periods in the high altitude. Moreover, the pressure to grow coca is great. Fortino needs the money and does not want problems with the drug lords. He believes that he cannot afford to worry about problems in the United States concerning the growing use of cocaine by younger and more widely dispersed groups.

Discussion Questions

1. How does Fortino's use of coca differ from the use of its processed product, cocaine, in the United States?
2. What are the implications of illicit drugs on socioeconomic and cultural development in agriculturally based regions, such as the Peruvian, Bolivian, and Colombian Andes? How can social development programs address alternatives to the profits made by growing illicit drugs in such regions?
3. In relation to the international production and consumption of illegal drugs, what can social workers, serving as agents of social development in the Andes Basin and in the United States, do in their respective countries to reduce the traffic in illicit drugs? What could they do together?

Vignette 2: Southern California

Jane and her roommate Carol ransack their apartment looking for their "works." Jane finds them on the floor next to a pizza box and some empty beer cans. She has just scored for the second time today and needs relief. After cooking the black tar (heroin), she ties off a vein in her leg and shoots up. The veins in her arm are already "burned." Despite nausea, Jane feels normal again. She will be "OK" for a while.

Jane has been through drug rehabilitation seven times. She and Carol support their habits by prostitution. Both have been raped and beaten several times. Jane thinks she probably has AIDS but is afraid to get tested. However, since she learned about the AIDS epidemic, she has stopped sharing needles and always insists that her clients use condoms.

Discussion Questions

1. Suppose you are a social work outreach worker. What strategies would you use to reach and work with someone such as Jane?
2. Beyond treatment and rehabilitation strategies, discuss practice approaches that may make life safer for a class of users such as Jane, as well as for other people who are at risk of falling into similar behaviors in the future.
3. Given the drug abuse–violence–maldevelopment complex evident in much of North American life, will schools of social work need to prepare future social workers any differently from the ways they did in the past? If so, in which ways? If not, why not?

Vignette 3: Romania

Violeta takes a sip of *tsuica*, Romanian plum brandy, to ease her hunger pains. Life has been difficult, with inflation running at 1,000 percent a year. The $150 she makes per month does not buy much meat at $2 a pound, particularly because she must pay $100 for her apartment and utilities. Life has been more complicated since all government subsidies for housing and utilities were eliminated. Of course, Violeta knows that drinking may not be good for her unborn child, but the pain of hunger is unbearable at times.

Besides, once she has a drink or two, she does not mind the beatings from her husband Mihai. Mihai hasn't been the same since his state job was eliminated as part of Romania's move to a market economy. Life will be easier for them both once they place their baby for adoption; the U.S. adoption agency they are working with has agreed to give them $2,000 for their baby if they both agree to relinquish the baby at birth.

Discussion Questions

1. How does the case of Violeta and Mihai differ from cases in the United States? How is it similar?
2. In your view, what is the relationship among alcohol consumption, violence, and maldevelopment in this case?
3. What type of cross-cultural practice model would you use to work with Violeta and Mihai and with other families who are experiencing similar problems in other parts of the world? Outline the processes in implementing the plan.

Exercise 2—Writing Assignment and Class Debate
Analysis of the Drug Problem

Purpose

To develop skills in analyzing different perspectives of the drug problem in the United States, developing one's own perspective, and convincing others about the necessity of taking action.

Issues to Be Addressed

What is the source of the drug problem—the supply (production) or the demand (consumption)? On the one hand, some people argue that the United States has a problem with illicit drugs because of the tremendous supply that is being produced in the global South and brought into this country. On the other hand, some people in the global South contend that the demand for drugs in the United States is the source of the problem and that if there were no demand for drugs, they would not produce the drugs.

Individual or Group Writing Assignment

Have the students write a position paper that consists of scholarly, well-reasoned arguments for each point of view based on the literature and including citations of all sources and then their own points of view. A student's own position may be one of the two discussed in the analysis or a well-developed alternative viewpoint, written in a scholarly and reflective way, to convince readers in general or a specific audience of the necessity of a particular course of action.

Classroom Debate

As an extension of the written assignment, conduct a debate in the classroom, with some students taking the "supply" position and some taking the "demand" position. Follow the debate with a presentation of alternative viewpoints and the class's decisions regarding the course or courses of action that governments, citizen groups, and helping professionals (especially social workers) need to take.

Other Suggested Assignments and Exercises

The following assignments and exercises, provided by the Midwest NASW Center on Violence, Development, and Substance Abuse (Illinois, Indiana, Michigan, and Ohio chapters), are recommended by curriculum area.

HUMAN BEHAVIOR IN THE SOCIAL ENVIRONMENT

1. Divide the class into three groups, each of which should examine the biopsychosocial effects of (a) the use or abuse of licit and illicit drugs, (b) violence, or (c) both a and b on human functioning at the individual, family, community, society, and international levels. Through the presentation of written and oral reports and subsequent discussions, the three groups can compare their results.
2. Explore alternative conceptions and models of social development and their usefulness in helping social workers to understand the com-

plex of drug abuse–violence–maldevelopment with a view to ameliorating the situation.

3. Compare the developmental issues facing the child of a poor farming family in Peru that grows coca for a living and a child growing up in poverty in the South Bronx of New York City whose family receives welfare. What role does violence play in each child's life? How are these two hypothetical children related to each other?

Social Work Theory and Practice

1. Show the film *Clear and Present Danger* (available on videocassette). In class or as a written assignment, have the students (a) identify the roles of policymakers and governmental officials in promulgating international drug trafficking; (b) extrapolate, from the film, the international, national, and community dynamics using a person-in-environment paradigm; and (c) extrapolate possible scenarios for practice in your community and for a family in the community.

2. Show a videotape of a film or have the students watch a scheduled television program on the interrelated topics of violence, poverty, drug trafficking, and drug abuse. Then conduct a class discussion on private problems versus public issues or diagnose the problem, identify its causes, and propose a treatment plan that includes changes at all levels (individual, family, community, society, and international).

3. Schedule a field trip to an economically underdeveloped area for observation and investigative reporting of the crime rate, housing conditions, economic conditions, health status, educational opportunities, and the prevalence and use of drugs in the area.

4. Plan a field visit to a hospital (a neonatal care unit or emergency room), a school in a low-income neighborhood, drug treatment centers (public and private), or a criminal justice center (a prison, police department, juvenile detention center, or court). Have the students write descriptive reports on the interrelationship of the issues involved in the drug abuse–violence–maldevelopment

complex of problems in the system they visited.

Social Welfare Policy

1. Have the students research U.S. policies on drug trafficking in the 1980s and compare them with the policies in the 1990s. Discuss which of the policies has been effective in dealing with the interrelationship among drug abuse, violence, and socioeconomic development, and why. What issues should new policies incorporate in addressing the interdependence of these issues?

2. Hold a class discussion on the following questions: What should be the role of social workers as change agents in advocating for policies on drug abuse, violence, and socioeconomic development? What can social work students do as students, practitioners, and citizens to bring about needed change with respect to the drug abuse–violence–maldevelopment complex of problems?

Research

1. Have the students review current newspaper articles, social work journals, and books to see what studies have been conducted on the relationship among socioeconomic conditions, violence, and drug abuse. Have them write a summary of two research articles that includes the identification of the problem, definition of concepts and variables, methodology (sample, procedure, data analysis), findings, limitations of the studies, and recommendations for further research.

2. Have the students interview concerned people (clinicians, administrators, and politicians) at different levels (city, county, state, and federal) to assess their awareness or knowledge of the drug abuse–violence–maldevelopment complex of problems.

Field Practicum

1. Ask the students to find out whether the community in which they are practicing has clearinghouses or other collaborative or

cooperative efforts to deal with the interrelationship of the problems of drug abuse, violence, and maldevelopment. Similarly, have them determine whether there are national or international resources and to enumerate them.

2. Have the students develop a strategic plan for reducing drug dependence and violence in a particular neighborhood, community, or city. What strategies might one use with the residents, politicians, and organizations in the development of the strategic plan to ensure its implementation?

FOR FURTHER READING

Billups, J. O. (1994). The social development model as an organizing framework for social work practice. In R. G. Meinert, J. T. Pardeck, & W. P. Sullivan (Eds.), *Issues in social work: A critical analysis* (pp. 21–37). Westport, CT: Aubury House.

This analysis of the recent literature, as well as of the profession's philosophy and mission, supports the conclusion that social workers need to use an integrative social development model to deal with the maldevelopment of people as it is manifested at various levels of human systems. That is, most practitioners need to pay less attention to individual and interpersonal remedies and more attention to community development, including socioeconomic systems that have an impact on the well-being of millions of people throughout the world.

Burke, A. C. (1995). Substance abuse: Legal issues. In R. L. Edwards (Ed.-in-Chief), *Encyclopedia of social work* (19th ed., Vol. 3, pp. 2347–2357). Washington, DC: NASW Press.

As this article makes clear,
drug policy in the last decade of the 20th century reflects a resurgence of antidrug sentiment and increased legal action aimed at limiting the availability and use of psychoactive substances. . . . Like more conventional wars, the War on Drugs has involved a massive mobilization of resources deployed in the name of national security. . . . By the end of the 1980s, military and policy forces had assumed a much larger role in opposing international drug production and trafficking. . . . (p. 2347)

[I]nterventions that stress the revitalization of communities' social and economic development address the need to offer community members positive alternative to drugs. (p. 2356)

Currie, E. (1993). *Reckoning: Drugs, the cities and the American future.* New York: Hill & Wang.

This book argues that the social roots of the drug crisis lie in the increasing disintegration of the economic and social structures of cities. It examines the uses and limits of traditional strategies—law enforcement, drug treatment, legalization—and proposes alternative interventions that are aimed at alleviating the underlying causes.

Morales, E. (1990). Comprehensive economic development: An alternative measure to reduce cocaine supply. *Journal of Drug Issues, 20,* 629–637.

Using data from published sources and from fieldwork in Peru, the largest cocaine-producing country, this article argues that the boom in the production of cocaine is the result of the political–economic relations between the global North and the global South. It contends that to wean Andean peasants from their dependence on the illicit cocaine economy, a comprehensive economic development program is necessary.

Narcotics and development. (1993). Washington, DC: Panos Institute.

This teaching–learning module presents an overview and history of illegal drugs and underdevelopment, discusses why poor farmers grow illegal drugs and the responses to the production, and argues that international drug policies and programs are required to deal with the causes of underdevelopment—poverty, unemployment, and hopelessness.

Philleo, J., & Brisbane, F. L. (1995). *Cultural competence for social workers: A guide for alcohol and other drug abuse prevention professionals working with ethnic/racial communities.* Rockville, MD: National Clearinghouse for Alcohol and Drug Information. (For a free copy, phone 800-729-6686; mention Order No. BKD 189)

This book presents research-based approaches to prevention that address the diverse needs of cultural and ethnic populations: African Americans, American Indians, Hispanics–Latinos, Pacific Islanders, and gay men and lesbians.

Salazar, L. S. (L. Fierro, trans.). (1993). "Drug trafficking" and social and political conflicts in Latin America. *Latin American Perspectives, 76,* 83–98.

The author states that a major problem that needs to be addressed is the misleading label "drug trafficking," as well as the Central American conflict, regional economic migration, and the vicissitudes of the democracies. He concludes that the "war on drugs" will continue because the nature of the drugs being used creates a marked tendency toward an increase in, or at least the stabilization of, the demand for drugs.

Tullis, L. (1991). *Handbook of research on the illicit drug traffic: Socioeconomic and political consequences* (UN Research Institute for Social Development). Westport, CT: Greenwood Press.

This handbook focuses on illicit drugs that are currently significant in international transactions: cocaine, heroin, and marijuana and other cannabis products. It presents information on the production, distribution, and consumption of these drugs and evaluates the intended, and sometimes unintended, consequences of various policies that are designed to deal with the socioeconomic and political effects of drug trafficking.

CHAPTER 5-2

DRUG ABUSE

EDUCATIONAL RESOURCE

The production, distribution, and consumption of illegal drugs has become one of the world's most corrosive threats, spawning crime and violence around the globe (UN, Development Programme, 1994). The problem has reached such proportions that the international retail value of illicit drugs now exceeds that of the world's oil trade and is second only to worldwide arms sales (King & Schneider, 1991).

The widespread international commerce in narcotics has flooded the United States with drugs that endanger individuals, families, and entire communities. Most of the contraband entering the country has been grown by poor farmers in the global South and processed and distributed by drug lords who wield enormous political and economic power (Shuman & Harvey, 1993).

Part 5 focuses primarily on cocaine and its derivative, crack. More than any other popular drug in U.S. history, crack cocaine has caused social damage on an unprecedented scale. It induces violent behavior in users and is linked with the unparalleled rise in crime and murder rates in the United States since its appearance on the streets in the 1980s (DuPont, 1991).

The world's cocaine-producing countries are Peru; Bolivia; Colombia; and, to a lesser extent, Ecuador and Brazil (*Narcotics and Development,* 1993). The main cocaine-consuming nation is the United States, which uses 75 percent of the world's cocaine (Office of National Drug Control Policy, 1995). Both the drug-producing and drug-consuming countries are linked in a cycle of sub-

stance abuse and violence. Because the drug problem is global, it cannot be solved by any one nation alone; rather, it requires a comprehensive and coordinated international response. The real solution to the drug crisis lies in eradicating one of its main root causes—poverty and the lack of viable economic opportunities—by promoting sustainable human development.

THE POWER OF CRACK COCAINE

Cocaine is a narcotic substance derived from the coca plant, a bushy shrub that is native to South America. The coca plant has been sacred to the Indian populations of the Andes since pre-Incan times because of its medicinal qualities. Cocaine is only one of 14 alkaloids contained in the coca leaf, which contains more than 28 nutrients that supplement the daily diets of many Andean people (*Narcotics and Development,* 1993).

The hallmark of crack cocaine is its ability to induce persistent, intensive drug-seeking behaviors. Studies of animals have shown that the reinforcing properties of cocaine are enormous, producing a powerful craving that leads the user to abandon everything to satisfy a compulsion to obtain more of the drug (DuPont, 1991). The intensity and rapid onset of euphoria, combined with a strong craving that may develop, account for crack cocaine's strong potential for addiction. The use of crack cocaine is concentrated primarily in high-risk, urban communities throughout the United States, where its sale in inexpensive single doses has widened its accessibility. The drug's low cost; ease of administration; and fast, powerful effects have made it a formidable street drug (DuPont, 1991).

Hundreds of thousands of people have become addicted to cocaine, particularly crack. Addiction should be viewed as a disease—not as a failure of individual willpower—from which many individuals can recover. Appropriate education can prevent some people from becoming addicted. For those who do become "hooked," treatment, not punishment, is the solution (Schmoke, 1990).

DRUG–RELATED VIOLENCE: A GLOBAL AFFLICTION

This section discusses the three elements of the narcotics chain—production, trafficking, and consumption—and the effects of drugs, both in the United States and in the global South.

Production

Poor farmers in the global South often cultivate the coca plant for drug production as a means of survival. Although they receive only 1 percent of the ultimate street price of the drugs they grow, the average $1,000 a year they can earn producing coca is often 25 percent to 50 percent more than what they can earn from growing such crops as bananas, corn, and oranges (UN Development Programme, 1994). As a farmer from Bolivia said, "I have no fear of what I am doing. I am obligated to plant this coca to take care of my five children" (Sims, 1995, p. A3).

The cultivation of coca is appealing to farmers for other reasons as well. Unlike other crops, the coca plant requires little care and is harvested only three times a year. In contrast, traditional crops require years of hard labor before they yield any fruit and are much heavier to transport through the jungle (Sims, 1995).

Along with the difficulty of growing food crops and the low income earned from doing so, farmers in the global South face other challenges, including the absence of long-term government support and armed conflicts that disrupt traditional planting practices and irrigation systems. At the international level, South American

countries face falling prices for typical exports, as well as an increasing international demand for illegal drugs (*Narcotics and Development,* 1993; Smith et al., 1992).

What happened in the Andes in the 1980s demonstrates how inadequate rural development contributes to the global drug crisis. After many mainstream agricultural initiatives to grow rubber, tobacco, coffee, and other crops failed, Colombian traffickers entered the Andes with coca seeds, demonstration plots, and venture capital, promising farmers that they would purchase their harvests. The Colombian cocaine "initiative" had a tremendous economic, social, and political impact on South America and the entire Western Hemisphere. Brazil experienced spiraling street crime as a result of cocaine consumption. Ecuador and Venezuela became centers for the laundering of drug money. Argentina saw an increase in drug traffickers, who exploited trade links with Europe. And Mexico and other countries became way stations en route to consumer markets, principally the United States (Smith et al., 1992).

Trafficking

Free trade and high-speed telecommunications have facilitated the smuggling of illicit narcotics out of the global South (Watson et al., 1993). Through an intricate network of drug-shipment routes and money-laundering bases, international drug-related crime organizations have managed to infiltrate countries around the world (Watson et al., 1993). Cooperation among such groups is increasing on an unprecedented scale (Atkinson, 1994). Moreover, these groups often have the help of legitimate organizations and individuals, including banks and other businesses and corrupt governmental officials (Andelman, 1994). During the summer of 1995, Colombia was rocked by allegations that its president, Ernesto Samper, had accepted nearly $6 million in campaign contributions from drug dealers in exchange for leniency in the courts. The Colombian defense minister resigned amid allegations that he had ordered a campaign treasurer to solicit money from major drug traffickers. "Political parties are losing credibility . . . the system itself is shaking," said

Francisco Thoumi, head of the Center for International Studies in Colombia (quoted in Schemo, 1995, p. 12).

The sale and use of narcotics in the global South has been accompanied by considerable violent crime. In Brazil, for example, gangs selling cocaine terrorize the *favelas* (slums) of Sao Paulo and Rio de Janeiro (Smith et al., 1992). In Colombia, 45 judges and 42 journalists were assassinated by drug thugs in the 1980s (Smith et al., 1992). In Mexico, drug traffickers are carving out an ever larger share of the world's drug trade. The bursts of violence that have attended the traffickers' rise have led many Mexicans to fear that their country is sliding toward the sort of terror the Medellin cocaine cartel unleashed on Colombia during the late 1980s and the early 1990s. From 1992 to 1995, victims have included the Roman Catholic cardinal of Guadalajara, two former state prosecutors, and more than a dozen active and retired federal police officers (Golden, 1995).

Narcotics trafficking has also had profound negative effects on entire economic systems by distorting local currencies, impeding foreign investments, depriving countries of tax revenues from traffickers, and discouraging legitimate development by offering higher wages than legal businesses (Smith et al., 1992).

As in the global South, narcotics trafficking has also created an alternative source of income in the United States. One of the most troubling results of the crack-cocaine craze has been the increase in violent gangs in American cities that are plagued by high unemployment, substandard educational systems, and the lack of services (Ostrowski, 1990). Forming an alternative economic system for people who otherwise feel shut out, the participation of gangs in the street cocaine trade creates an illegal source of revenue for people of all ages, even nine-year-old children who earn $100 a day serving as lookouts for dealers (Rohr, 1990). At the same time, the drug trade constrains legitimate economic development by fueling crime and violence.

When the sale and use of narcotics creates social turmoil, the institutional response of the police or military is often increased repressive violence (Van Soest & Bryant, 1995). For example, to wage the "War on Drugs," U.S. police SWAT teams and paramilitary task forces carry out sweeps in housing projects and mass evictions of drug suspects and their families. There have even been calls for deploying the National Guard and federal troops to patrol ghetto "war zones" (*Narcotics and Development*, 1993).

Consumption

As Representative Charles B. Rangel (D-NY) (quoted in Benjamin, 1990) eloquently stated:

> We have watched many of our young kids turn to dope to cope because they are without hope. America has watched and wept as many lives have become twisted and snuffed out by the powerful lure of drug addiction. (p. 82)

Drug consumption is at the other end of the narcotics chain. Most drug users and abusers live in the industrialized countries of the global North. In the United States, over 6 million users spent $31 billion on cocaine and crack in 1993 (Office of National Drug Control Policy, 1995). Their behavior often has enormous social, economic, and political consequences not only for them and their families but for society in general. On a monetary basis alone, drug-related crime, law enforcement, health care, and treatment cost the United States an estimated $29.1 billion a year (U.S. Department of Justice, 1994). Among violent offenders in state prisons, 50 percent reported being under the influence of alcohol or drugs at the time they committed the offenses, and 79 percent reported using drugs previously (U.S. Department of Justice, 1994).

Drug abuse is not limited to the global North, however. In recent years, some countries in the global South have experienced a dramatic increase in the consumption of hard drugs, particularly among young men in urban areas. The risk of drug addiction is particularly high in source countries, where cheap drugs are readily available. Many urban areas of the global South have several of the same troubling characteristics that thrive in parts of the United States: high unemployment, the lack of services, and inadequate or nonexistent educational opportunities (Smith et al., 1992).

A serious threat in the Andean region is the smoking of a mixture of coca paste and tobacco—called *pitillo* in Peru and Bolivia and *basuco* in Colombia—which can cause quick addiction and permanent brain damage because of the high concentration of chemical impurities in the drug. Colombia is estimated to have as many as 500,000 basuco smokers, mostly unemployed youths and other marginalized people (Smith et al., 1992).

Around the world, substance abuse has created additional victims. Unlike other drugs, crack cocaine quickly achieved a high rate of use and addiction among pregnant women and women of childbearing age. Its use has resulted in hundreds of thousands of drug-exposed babies, who are frequently born premature and suffering from damage to their nervous systems or have other complications (DuPont, 1991).

CASE STUDIES

The following two studies exemplify two different backgrounds where illegal drugs are used.

CASE STUDY 1
Weasel and the Logan 30

Weasel strolls down Logan Avenue amid scores of drug users, buyers, and sellers. He is pleased because his gang, the Logan 30, is making lots of money. Most of the drug users ignore Weasel, but the sellers are aware of his presence and are nervously deferential. Most of the drug sellers are addicts themselves, although some are just youngsters hoping to be as successful as Weasel. None of the sellers can afford to alienate Weasel.

Across the trash-strewn street, Mrs. Yoder looks out her apartment window with a mixture of disgust and fear. Although this street had always been poor, the neighborhood was clean and safe until a few years ago. Neighbors used to talk to each other and look out for one another. There was no graffiti and there were no shootings. The street lights worked, and the trash was picked up weekly. The Logan 30 was just a group of kids hanging out together back then. Like many of her longtime neighbors, Mrs. Yoder wonders how things got so out of hand. "Didn't the police and the city care about them?" She closes the blinds and watches the door.

Weasel is on a mission. He meets Shooter at the corner liquor store, which serves as the neighborhood's only source of food. There are no grocery stores anymore; bread and milk cost twice as much here as they do in the suburbs, and malt liquor is cheaper than soda. Weasel and Shooter pick up a package from the clerk, who tells them that it just arrived from Mexico and "hasn't been stepped on" yet. Shooter samples the package's contents while Weasel watches the door.

A police car slowly rolls up the street. For a moment, all but the most brazen drug dealers cease business. Officers Miller and Sanders watch. They know that as soon as they turn the corner, the drug market will return to life. Although they will make several arrests tonight, they know they will not make a dent in the illicit activities. They are frustrated and burned out. As they watch the users and sellers patiently wait, a call comes in on the radio. There's been a shooting at an apartment complex not far away. The police car speeds off with its lights flashing.

Hearing the nearby gunshots, Weasel and Shooter check their own guns. Their package is worth more than most people earn in a year, and they won't let their rivals take it without a fight. Guns are their only form of insurance, and violence unfortunately is a business necessity. Weasel and Shooter carefully walk down the street and distribute their product. When they finish, they will meet the rest of the Logan 30 in an abandoned house down the street. After they count the day's profits, the group will party into the next morning, getting high on drugs and alcohol (case study provided by the Midwest NASW Center on Violence, Development, and Substance Abuse).

CASE STUDY 2
Julie

Julie wakes up at 7:45 A.M. feeling slightly nauseated and with a headache from overdrinking and using cocaine at a party the night before. She will be late for work again (which makes twice this week) and is annoyed with herself for waking up late. She lights a cigarette and stumbles to the bathroom, reassuring herself that her boss will overlook her tardiness because she had a stellar performance review and has a solid attendance record. Julie views her occasional party nights as a means of compensating for her hard work and as a source of adventure in her otherwise mundane life.

At 26, Julie is the youngest corporate attorney at her company. She had no problem landing a high-paying job at the Fortune 500 company because she is a graduate of an Ivy League university and has great credentials. Julie enjoys the after-hour rituals that she and her colleagues have established to reward themselves for their accomplishments. After a hard day's work, they gather at the local bar for drinks (and sometimes cocaine on the side) and stimulating conversations before they head home. Julie enjoys feeling "buzzed" and carefree.

Julie began drinking beer and wine and smoking cigarettes in high school. In college she first experimented with marijuana and gradually moved on to other drugs, such as cocaine and ecstacy. As with her use of alcohol and cigarettes, Julie manages to confine her experimentation with drugs exclusively to social occasions. Besides hangovers, until now Julie has suffered no noticeable negative physical or social consequences from her use of substances. She believes that her use of illicit drugs is no different from her use of legal drugs.

Julie has always been a strong advocate for legalizing the sale and use of drugs. She thinks that the current U.S. drug laws are, at best, based on moralistic assumptions and that they are hypocritical, economics driven, and manipulated by political demagogues. When Julie debates this issue with friends, she points out that altering one's perception through the use of natural drugs is a behavior that has been part of virtually every culture since the earliest societies. Furthermore, the consequences of getting high are often determined by the social context, values, and norms of a society anyway. Julie concedes, however, that substance use is a problem for some people and could have dangerous consequences, such as accidents, crime, and violence. But, she argues, the War on Drugs is hypocritical in a society that legally consumes billions of dollars worth of alcohol and tobacco each year. Moreover, the U.S. government subsidizes these industries' efforts to sell their products overseas to the so-called Third World countries (case study provided by the Midwest NASW Center on Violence, Development, and Substance Abuse).

ONE SOURCE OF HOPE: THE ENTREPRENEURIAL DEVELOPMENT INSTITUTE

The primary goal of the Entrepreneurial Development Institute (TEDI), based in Washington, DC, is to equip youths and their families in that city with the skills and resources necessary to become full stakeholders in the economic and social revitalization of their communities by establishing their own small businesses (TEDI, 1995). TEDI has a microloan fund available to students who have completed the first part of the training program and are ready to start their own businesses. Since 1991, 1,800 youths have been involved, and 85 business plans have been drawn up, creating over 650 jobs (personal communication with TEDI staff, August 1996). Of the adjudicated youths who make up 30 percent of the participants, TEDI boasts an amazing zero percent recidivism rate for drug-related offenses. Parents, teachers, and counselors claim that TEDI graduates get better grades, act more responsibly at home, and engage in long-term educational and career planning. TEDI proves that entrepreneurial education is a viable alternative to drugs and crime, a means of achieving economic self-sufficiency, and a pathway to academic excellence. TEDI is now planning to replicate its model in 18 other cities across the country.

CURTAILING DRUG–RELATED VIOLENCE THROUGH SUSTAINABLE HUMAN DEVELOPMENT

Development alone will not be the solution to the narcotics problem, but it does provide a more adequate platform for dealing with the underlying causes. (Smith et al., 1992, p. 114)

The 1980s were characterized by the unrestrained consumption of resources by the rich countries of the global North, which intensified worldwide injustices and poverty. One result has been increasing alienation and loss of hope that fuel the use of drugs and violence (Korten, 1990). Sustainable human development, as an antidote to hopelessness, is the most effective means of getting at the root causes of the drug problem and reducing the production, trafficking, and consumption of illegal drugs.

Reducing Production

As Shuman and Harvey (1993) pointed out, a key reason why the aggressive law enforcement approach favored by the United States has not been effective is that it fails to recognize that growers have a different motive from international traffickers: survival. Poor farmers grow coca plants primarily because producing drug crops yields higher profits and guaranteed markets and hence provides an alternative to the abject poverty and governmental neglect that have plagued their communities for decades.

To curb production, farmers must have viable alternative ways of earning a decent living. Replacing coca with other agricultural produce will not be sufficient. Rather, ensuring the successful substitution of food crops for coca will depend on several factors, including local marketing systems that protect perishable crops; transportation to markets; steady buyers; the allowance of sufficient time for the new crops to take hold; and international policies that provide favorable trade, credit, infrastructure, and price conditions (*Narcotics and Development*, 1993).

According to the United Nations Development Pro-gramme (1994), it is unreasonable to expect the global South to bear most of the cost of clamping down on the production and export of illegal drugs because demand in the global North fuels the narcotics trade. Rather, the UN has recommended that countries in the global North should be generous in supporting sustainable human development programs for poor farmers, including assistance for farm equipment and small-scale loans.

Reducing Trafficking

International interdiction of narcotics trafficking has been minimally successful to date and requires a different approach. Currently, nations rely on primitive law enforcement networks to eradicate crops, to prevent large-scale laundering of drug profits, and to prosecute drug lords. In the absence of serious enforceable international drug laws, criminals simply move freely to countries with the weakest antidrug policies (Shuman & Harvey, 1993).

In the United States, youths will find it hard to resist the lure of the drug trade as long as they can make a hundred times more by selling drugs than by working at minimum-wage jobs that offer no health benefits and no chance of promotion. A social development approach is needed to combat the problem. Such an approach requires adequate educational opportunities, economic programs to bring businesses and industries back to poor communities, and improved community resources and infrastructure to support the healthy development of individuals and neighborhoods.

Reducing Consumption

Because drug addiction is a disease (and because drug-related crime is often associated with feeding addictions), the focus should be on preventing and treating substance abuse. A federally funded study by the RAND Corporation found that drug treatment is seven times more cost-effective in cutting the demand for cocaine than are local law enforcement efforts, 11 times more effective than border interdiction, and 22 times more effective than efforts to control foreign production ("Focus on Drug Treatment," 1994).

One drastic proposal put forth to reduce the consumption of illicit drugs is legalization. This is a risky proposition, however, because consumption may actually increase. Ultimately, the best solution seems to be to promote social and economic development in the global North and South as a means of strengthening families and communities, providing alternatives to drug use, and offering hope (UN Development Programme, 1994).

Funding Sustainable Human Development Strategies

Curtailing the drug epidemic requires long-term, multifaceted approaches that address its root causes. Implementing such approaches undoubtedly would be expensive. The irony is that the United States and the entire international community end up paying in any case—and they pay a lot more down the line than they would have paid up front (UN Development Programme, 1994). For $25 billion, which is half the cost American cities are now paying to curb crime, sickness, and other damages from the War on Drugs, the United States could pay every rural family in Latin America $1,000, the typical annual income for a coca farmer, not to grow coca (Shuman & Harvey, 1993).

Providing money for development in both the source countries of the global South and in underdeveloped areas in the consumer countries of the global North requires a change of priorities. The UN Development Programme (1994) proposed a 3 percent reduction in global military spending from 1995 to 2000, which would produce $85 billion in new funds for sustainable human development throughout the world. For development programs to succeed, however, they must meet the basic human needs of every person, expand economic opportunities for poor people, promote meaningful citizen participation, and protect the environment (*At the Crossroads*, 1995).

WHAT YOU CAN DO

- Learn more about the interdependent causes and consequences of the maldevelopment–substance abuse–violence cycle, using the information and references in part 5 as a start.

- Learn about solutions to the drug problem that focus on international cooperation to reduce both the supply and demand of illicit drugs.
- Develop a greater understanding of international development issues and use that understanding to advocate for programs that address the root causes of the drug problem: poverty and inequity.
- Advocate for the worldwide reduction in military expenditures to free up resources for development.

REFERENCES

Andelman, D. A. (1994). The drug money maze. *Foreign Affairs, 73,* 994–1008.

At the crossroads: The future of foreign aid (Occasional Paper No. 4). (1995). (Available from Bread for the World Institute, 1100 Wayne Avenue, Suite 1000, Silver Spring, MD 20910; phone 301-608-2400)

Atkinson, R. (1994, June 28). FBI chief urges Europeans to shift cold war resources to fight crime. *Washington Post,* p. A18.

Benjamin, P. (1990). A war on drugs can reduce violence in black neighborhoods. In J. Rohr (Ed.), *Violence in America: Opposing viewpoints* (pp. 80–85). San Diego: Greenhaven Press.

DuPont, R. (Ed.). (1991). *Crack cocaine: A challenge for prevention.* Washington, DC: U.S. Department of Health and Human Services.

Entrepreneurial Development Institute. (1995). *General organization overview.* (Available from the institute at 2025 I Street, NW, Suite 905, Washington, DC 20006; phone 202-822-8334)

Focus on drug treatment. (1994, June 16). *USA Today,* p. A12.

Golden, T. (1995, July 30). Mexican connection grows as cocaine supplier to U.S. *New York Times,* p. A1.

King, A., & Schneider, B. (1991). *The first global revolution.* New York: Pantheon Books.

Korten, D. (1990). *Getting to the 21st century: Voluntary actions and the global agenda.* West Hartford, CT: Kumarian Press.

Narcotics and development. (1993). Washington, DC: Panos Institute.

Office of National Drug Control Policy. (1995). *What America's users spend on illegal drugs, 1988–1993.* Washington, DC: Executive Office of the President.

Ostrowski, J. (1990). Repealing drug laws can reduce drug violence. In J. Rohr (Ed.), *Violence in America: Opposing viewpoints* (pp. 73–79). San Diego: Greenhaven Press.

Rohr, J. (1990). Preface to Chapter 2. In J. Rohr (Ed.), *Violence in America: Opposing viewpoints* (pp. 50–51). San Diego: Greenhaven Press.

Schemo, D. J. (1995, August 13). Colombia in crisis as drugs tar chief. *New York Times,* p. A12.

Schmoke, K. L. (1990). More law enforcement cannot reduce drug violence. In J. Rohr (Ed.), *Violence in America: Opposing viewpoints* (pp. 59–66). San Diego, CA: Greenhaven Press.

Shuman, M. H., & Harvey, H. (1993). *Security without war: A post–cold war foreign policy.* Boulder, CO: Westview Press.

Sims, C. (1995, July 11). Defying U.S. threat, Bolivians plant more coca. *New York Times,* p. A3.

Smith, M. L., Thongtham, C. N., Sadeque, N., Bravo, A. M., Rumrill, R., & Davila, A. (1992). *Why people grow drugs: Narcotics and development in the Third World.* Washington, DC: Panos Institute.

United Nations Development Programme. (1994). *Human development report, 1994.* New York: Oxford University Press.

U.S. Department of Justice. (1994). *Drugs and crime facts, 1994.* Washington, DC: U.S. Government Printing Office.

Van Soest, D., & Bryant, S. (1995). Violence reconceptualized for social work: The urban dilemma. *Social Work, 40,* 549–557.

Watson, R., Katel, P., Gutkin, S., Waller, D., Liu, M., & Spencer, R. (1993, December 13). Death on the spot: The end of a drug king. *Newsweek,* pp. 19–21.

ADDITIONAL RESOURCES

National Clearinghouse for Alcohol and
  Drug Information
PO Box 2345
Rockville, MD 20852
Phone: 800-729-6686
  A government agency that collects and provides information about narcotics in the United States.

Panos Institute
1025 T. Jefferson Street, NW, Suite 105
Washington, DC 20007
Phone: 202-965-5177
  A research institute that publishes educational materials on issues of development, including the narcotics trade.

PART 6

TRAUMA
_____

SURVIVAL IS VICTORY

CHAPTER 6-1

TRAUMA

CURRICULUM

Part 6 addresses the relationship between trauma and violence and provides opportunities to learn from strategies that are used to heal victims of trauma.

GENERAL OBJECTIVES

1. Students will be able to describe parallel conditions of violence in the United States and in less economically advantaged nations.
2. Students will demonstrate a broadened understanding of violence and the role of the social work profession in solving the problem on a global scale.
3. Students will demonstrate an increased interest in learning from successful interventions undertaken by human services workers in the global South and in the United States.
4. Students will be able to define key concepts, such as sustainable human development, global North, and global South.
5. Students will demonstrate an awareness of social work's commitment to social justice by describing how violence and oppression affect vulnerable populations throughout the world.

The objectives and discussion questions in the following section are presented by curricular area. The questions may be used for classroom discussions or in written assignments. They are based on information presented in part 6 of *An Educational Resource* (pp. 113–120 in this volume and pp. 47–54 in the student version).

HUMAN BEHAVIOR IN THE SOCIAL ENVIRONMENT

Objectives

1. Students will demonstrate a greater understanding of the impact and interrelationship of violence-related trauma on the individual, family, and community.
2. Students will be able to describe how unresolved trauma and the resulting cycle of violence impede individual and community development.

Discussion Questions

1. If left untreated, trauma can block the development of individuals at any stage of the life cycle. What are three common responses of traumatized individuals? Give an example of each response based on your work with clients in your field placement or from other experiences.
2. Describe how unresolved trauma may affect the processes of both individual and community development. How are the two related? For instance, how do traumatized individuals influence community development, and how do traumatized communities influence individual development?

SOCIAL WORK THEORY AND PRACTICE

Objectives

1. Students will be able to describe strategies used in the global South that are aimed at

achieving justice and equity and at healing trauma.

2. Students will be able to describe some unique ways in which ethnic communities have provided for healing from loss and trauma through their rituals and traditions.

3. Students will demonstrate an understanding of the necessity of developing processes of healing with victims and perpetrators to prevent the cycle of violence from continuing.

4. Students will demonstrate an understanding of the dynamics of posttraumatic stress disorder (PTSD) and strategies for intervention.

Discussion Questions

1. Part 6 of *An Educational Resource* (pp. 115–116 in this volume and pp. 49–50 in the student version) presents several approaches to healing. Consider a situation with which you are familiar (either directly or indirectly) that involved violence-related trauma (for example, an abused child, a battered woman, a crime-infested neighborhood, or a community shaken by a hate crime). Which of the approaches, if any, would be applicable to that situation? Discuss strategies that may promote healing in that situation.

2. In working with refugee children and families, what are some important issues related to violence and trauma that should be considered? What are some specific techniques and strategies that social workers may use?

SOCIAL WELFARE POLICY

Objectives

1. Students will demonstrate an understanding of violence-related trauma and the need for responses that focus on global interdependence, the elimination of poverty, and the need for world justice and equity.

2. Students will demonstrate an awareness that trauma is an obstacle to human, social, and economic development.

Discussion Questions

1. What are some implications for policies and programs that social services agencies should

consider with regard to issues of unresolved trauma and the cycle of violence?

2. Discuss the three levels of violence—personal, institutional, and structural—in relationship to developing agency programs for working with immigrants and refugees (see part 6 of *An Educational Resource*, pp. 113–114 of this volume and pp. 47–48 of the student version). Which factors should be part of a comprehensive program? Which of the approaches to healing presented in part 6 of *An Educational Resource* (pp. 115–116 in this volume and pp. 49–50 in the student version) may be useful, and how?

RESEARCH

Objectives

1. Students will be aware of and understand the complexity of the interrelations of trauma issues related to individual, family, and community development.

2. Students will examine research studies that explore the connections between trauma-related violence and international development and between trauma-related violence and development in the United States.

Discussion Questions

1. Part 6 of *An Educational Resource* (pp. 114–115 in this volume and pp. 48–49 in the student version) discusses three common responses of traumatized individuals. What does the research literature related to one of the three responses have to say? Be sure that you examine studies from other countries, as well as those conducted in the United States.

2. Which studies that are cited in part 6 of *An Educational Resource* present findings on what can be learned from strategies that are used in other countries to help people and communities heal from violence-related trauma?

FIELD PRACTICUM

Objectives

1. Students will recognize the long-term, negative consequences of psychosocial trauma and

of the oppression of people and the need to counteract such consequences by working to eliminate oppression.

2. Students will be able to describe specific healing approaches that have been successful in addressing the consequences of violence-related trauma in other countries and to explore ways to replicate them in U.S. communities.

Discussion Questions

1. Which interventions may be used to stop the cycle of violence in a family in which there is child abuse or battering and with a violent youth?
2. How can social workers keep from becoming traumatized themselves when working with traumatized clients?

Exercise 1—Classroom Discussion
Vignettes

Purpose

To raise awareness of the traumatic effects of different kinds of violence to which people are exposed worldwide.

Learning Activity

Ask the students to read the following 13 vignettes aloud in the classroom in a round-robin manner as a means of stimulating discussion of and raising issues about violence-related trauma. Then discuss the questions that appear following the vignettes. (The vignettes may be copied for classroom use.)

Vignette 1: A seven-year-old boy scavenging for rice in Rwanda was shot dead by soldiers who assumed he was an insurgent.

Vignette 2: A young child in El Salvador was shot and killed by a drunk paramilitary soldier who was known in the neighborhood as an alcoholic and a bully.

Vignette 3: Thinking that rebels were inside, soldiers shot into a hut in Vietnam during the Vietnam War, killing a pregnant woman and her husband and leaving their young child, who was wounded and bleeding profusely, to die.

Vignette 4: Gang members in Washington, DC, aiming at rival gang members, shot a five-year-old girl while she was swimming in the neighborhood pool.

Vignette 5: A group of five children in Cambodia found an unexploded cluster bomb. Although the children knew it was a bomb, they attempted to dismantle it. The bomb exploded, killing all but one boy, who was blinded.

Vignette 6: In Illinois, two four-year-old boys who were best friends found a gun in the house and, while playing, one of them shot the other. When the father ran to see what the noise was about, he found the boy who was alive in a comatose state staring at the blood-covered body of his friend.

Vignette 7: Some 20,000 people in Angola and 50,000 people in Mozambique have had limbs amputated as a result of conflicts in these countries.

Vignette 8: In violence-riddled neighborhoods in the United States, many young men are wheelchair bound because of gun injuries. In some cases, it is seen as a badge of honor to have been disabled or jailed.

Vignette 9: Between 1987 and 1991, thousands of underage boys in Ethiopia were taken by the military, in sweeps of public places and without notifying their parents, and were given little training before they were deployed directly to the fighting front.

Vignette 10: In the mid-1980s, some mothers, who lived under poor conditions in camps for displaced persons in El Salvador, were convinced to give up their youngest children to families in other countries. They were given an equivalent of about $40 U.S. by unscrupulous people who managed "fattening houses" and illegal adoption services. Children were also kidnapped for the same purpose.

Vignette 11: "Sometimes my daughter or my son has barely done something wrong, I mean nothing, and I start shouting at them. Screaming. I beat them. Then, I mean, my heart, I don't know how, it gets sort of a cramp. I say, 'Why did I hit them? Why did I do that?' I start doing my own trial" —A Lebanese mother.

Vignette 12: "His hair here is white since then, and since that day he gets scared. . . . Is it that since that day he gets these suffocations? I don't know. He stays like this . . . he doesn't talk to anybody. He doesn't sit while anyone is here. . . . He often sits alone, spaced out. He spaces out a lot." —A Lebanese mother's description of her 11-year-old son after he was threatened with execution by unknown soldiers.

Vignette 13: A 17-year-old boy saw a friend killed and his body burned by opposition forces in the civil war in Sri Lanka. He became distraught and lost control of his bladder.

Discussion Questions

1. What were your feelings and thoughts after you heard the various vignettes?
2. What are the different types of violence described in the stories? What do the vignettes have in common?
3. The vignettes represent situations from many parts of the world. Why are international examples provided? What are the connections between those examples and situations in the United States?
4. Why is it important for social workers to become aware of such stories when they are so dreadful?
5. Discuss strategies for rehabilitation and prevention in cases of violence-related trauma. Are there any approaches that may be applicable worldwide?

Exercise 2—Writing Assignment
Working with Traumatized Refugee Children

Learning Objectives

To stimulate discussion of the effects of war on children and to identify the need for further knowledge and skills for effective practice with refugees.

Learning Activity

The following case example can be used as learning material on several levels, from sensitizing students to the refugee experience to assessing the symptoms of PTSD in clinical practice.

Case Study: An Initial Interview with H

Ask the students to read the case study of the interview with H in part 6 of *An Educational Resource* (pp. 116–117 in this volume and pp. 50–51 in the student version). Then ask them to address the following questions in an essay. The questions may also be used to stimulate in-class discussion.

Discussion Questions

1. If you were working with H, what further data would you collect?
2. How would you go about establishing a relationship with H?
3. After this initial interview, you would have a conference with your supervisor. What issues or concerns would you raise with the supervisor about H?
4. What is your assessment of PTSD at this point? What symptoms are there?

Exercise 3—Developing Intervention Strategies for Traumatized Children and Their Families

Purpose

To help students develop skills in assessing and developing intervention approaches to help children and families heal from violence-related trauma.

Learning Activity

Choose a neighborhood, community, or country in which violence is pervasive. The violence may involve national conflicts, such as a civil war, state violence against citizens, violence against racial and ethnic groups, civil disorders and disturbances, or ethnic conflict; international conflicts, such as a conventional war; an area in which there is a high rate of violent crime like homicides, assaults, or domestic violence; or structural violence, such as conditions of poverty, homelessness, and discrimination.

Ask the students to write a three-part development plan that includes the following:
- Part 1—a description of the community
- Part 2—an assessment of the psychosocial distress
- Part 3—development of a plan for intervention strategies.

Full Instructions to Students

(This exercise may be copied for classroom use.)

Part 1: Describe the neighborhood, community, or country that you have chosen. Provide demographic information related to the population and the conditions of violence.

Part 2: Assess the conditions of psychosocial distress in the community by answering the questions in the following areas:

FACTS
1. Are children being protected, cared for, and nurtured to meet the essential psychological and social needs for normal growth and development and for any special needs created by traumatic experiences?
2. Which children have unfulfilled psychological and social needs that deserve special consideration?
3. What deprivations, circumstances, or experiences are causing these needs?
4. What resources exist and what efforts are being made by the children, their caregivers, and community-resource persons to meet these needs?

RISK
1. Which children are at risk of not having their essential psychological and social needs met, are in deleterious circumstances, or are likely to experience traumatic events that will affect their psychosocial well-being?

PREVENTION
1. What measures are required to ensure that children receive essential care and nurturing for normal psychosocial development and to prevent or minimize possible psychosocial trauma?

RESPONSE
1. At the time of a traumatic event or psychosocial distress, what special psychological and social needs are children and their families likely to have?
2. What emergency assistance would contribute to the ability of parents and community-resource persons to meet those needs?

PREPAREDNESS
1. What advance measures could families and other interveners take to ensure that assistance measures would be effective during an emergency?

REHABILITATION
1. After a traumatic experience or distressing incident, what short-term measures could be taken to help children and their families to cope?

RECOVERY
1. What measures are required to facilitate the healthy psychological and social recovery of children who have survived traumatic experiences?

Part 3: Develop a multifaceted program that addresses the needs assessed in each area in Part 2. The interventions that you propose should be guided by the following principles:

1. Focus intervention efforts on individuals' coping strengths and psychosocial well-being, not simply on distress and injury.
2. Strive to ensure that a child has a need-fulfilling environment, considering the totality of the child in the contexts of his or her family, community, and society.
3. Give priority to helping families care for and protect their children.
4. Be sensitive to the particular meanings that traumatic experiences may have in the culture.
5. Stress culturally appropriate interventions, using local resource people when possible.
6. Ensure that appropriate psychosocial interventions are introduced in a timely manner.
7. Ensure that the interventions chosen are appropriately age specific.
8. Use supportive interventions for children that cause the least harm and do not retraumatize them.
9. Ensure that the psychosocial needs of all children are met, regardless of which side of a conflict they, their families, or their communities may be on.
10. Avoid institutionalizing or removing distressed children from their families or communities for treatment.
11. Encourage the prevention of psychological difficulties by stimulating social interaction, cultural activities, and religious practices.
12. Respect the wishes and sensitivities of people who have survived traumatic experiences, ensuring that they have opportunities to fulfill their needs without being forced to talk about topics on which they wish to remain silent.

Source: Ressler, Tortorici, & Marcelino, 1993, pp. 204–205.

Exercise 4—Classroom Discussion
Case Studies of Healing from
Violence-Related Trauma

The Circle of Healing

Ask the students to read the Circle of Healing case study in part 6 of *An Educational Resource* (p. 117 in this volume and p. 51 in the student version). Then ask them to consider the following questions.
1. What are the factors that go into the Circle of Healing?
2. What are the strengths of the model presented?
3. Would such an approach work in your community? Why or why not?
4. What are the implications of the case study for social work intervention?

Ms. G

Ask the students to read the case study of Ms. G in part 6 of *An Educational Resource* (pp. 117–118 in this volume and pp. 51–52 in the student version). Then ask them to consider the following questions.
1. What are some of the sources of the trauma Ms. G may be experiencing, including those from her country of origin and those in the United States?
2. Part 6 of *An Educational Resource* (pp. 114–115 in this volume and pp. 48–49 in the student version) presents some of the effects of unresolved trauma on development. What seems to be Ms. G's response to the violence she has experienced?
3. What approaches did the social worker use to help Ms. G begin to heal?

Exercise 5—Writing Assignment
A Program for Traumatized Mozambican
Women and Children

Ask the students to read the case study in part 6 of *An Educational Resource* about the programs established in Zambia for Mozambican women and children (p. 118 in this volume and p. 52 in the student version). Then ask them to address the following questions in an essay. The questions may also be used for in-class discussion.
1. What are the key elements of the program described in the case example?
2. Do you think that the major aspects of the program—targeting women as well as children, empowerment, education, healing, and community development—are important in helping children heal from violence-related trauma? If so, how and why?

3. How could the program be adapted to violence-infested neighborhoods in the United States?

REFERENCE

Ressler, E. M., Tortorici, J. M., & Marcelino, A. (1993). *Children in war: A guide to the provision of services.* New York: UNICEF.

FOR FURTHER READING

Cattell-Gordon, D. (1990). The Appalachian inheritance: A culturally transmitted traumatic stress syndrome? *Journal of Progressive Human Services, 1*(1), 41–56.

This article examines the concept of a culturally transmitted traumatic stress syndrome induced by exploitation and oppression, on the basis of a study of victims of chronic unemployment in Appalachia. It has abroad implications for many different groups, including Native Americans and African Americans whose forced captivity resulted in traumatization and homeless children.

The following books and articles—written, coauthored, or edited by Charles Figley, professor, School of Social Work, Florida State University, Tallahassee, and director of the university's Marriage and Family Therapy Center—are recommended for further reading:

1978. Delayed stress response syndrome: Family therapy implications (with D. H. Sprenkle). *Journal of Marriage and Family Counseling, 4,* 53–60.

1978. *Stress disorders among Vietnam veterans: Theory, research, and treatment.* New York: Brunner/ Mazel.

1980. *Strangers at home: Vietnam veterans since the war* (edited with S. Leventman). New York: Praeger.

1983. *Stress and the family: Vol. 2. Coping with catastrophe* (edited with H. I. McCubbin). New York: Brunner/Mazel.

1985. *Trauma and its wake: The study and treatment of post-traumatic stress disorder.* New York: Brunner/ Mazel.

1986. *Trauma and its wake: Vol. 2. Traumatic stress disorder—Theory, research, and treatment.* New York: Brunner/Mazel.

1989. *Treating stress in families.* New York: Brunner/ Mazel.

1991. Critical services for the veterans of the Gulf War. In Department of Veterans Affairs, VA Persian Gulf Returnees Working Group, *War zone stress among returning Persian Gulf troops: A preliminary report* (pp. D3–D14). West Haven, CT: National Center for PTSD.

1993. Coping with stressors on the home front. *Journal of Social Issues, 49*(4), 51–71.

1993. Intervention with families and children of the troops: War-related secondary traumatic stress. In L. A. Levitt & N. A. Fox (Eds.), *Psychological effect of war and violence on children* (pp. 184–196). Hillsdale, NJ: Lawrence Erlbaum.

1993. Weathering the storm at home: Gulf War-related family stress and coping. In F. Kaslow (Ed.), *The military family in peace and war* (pp. 173–190). New York: Springer.

1995. *Compassion fatigue: Secondary traumatic stress disorder from helping the traumatized.* New York: Brunner/Mazel.

Ressler, E. M., Tortorici, J. M., & Marcelino, A. (1993). *Children in war: A guide to the provision of services.* New York: UNICEF.

This book is a short, generic (that is, not specific to any country), and practical summary of the various impacts of conflict on children (loss of life; injury, illness, malnutrition, and disability; torture, abuse, imprisonment, recruitment; loss of family members; psychosocial distress; and disruption of education), what is being done to counter these effects, and the need for comprehensive planning and programming.

CHAPTER 6-2

TRAUMA

EDUCATIONAL RESOURCE

Rwandans fleeing the mass killing in their village are emotionally numb by the time they reach the border with Zaire. A Vietnam War veteran abuses alcohol and cannot hold down a job. A child becomes withdrawn and takes no interest in her schoolwork after her family is forced to move to a homeless shelter. Across national borders, people who have been traumatized share many of the same symptoms. All have experienced or witnessed overwhelming violence, whether it is structural violence (such as poverty, hunger, and homelessness), personal violence (such as mugging and rape), or institutional violence (such as war, genocide, state repression, and torture).

Part 6 explores three causes of trauma and the relationship between trauma and violence. It also examines strategies that have been used both in the United States and in the global South to heal victims of trauma.

WHAT IS TRAUMA?

Exposure to sudden, prolonged, or repeated experiences of a life-threatening nature may result in deep emotional wounding, or psychological trauma, for victims and witnesses. Such emotional injury often includes feelings of intense rage and powerlessness. The scenes and images of violence become permanently imprinted in the psyche, along with associated feelings of terror and anguish (Prigoff, 1995).

Posttraumatic stress disorder (PTSD) is a psychological condition that results from exposure to a traumatic experience that exceeds a person's ability to respond or cope effectively. Symptoms associated with PTSD include flashbacks (in which the victim repeatedly reexperiences the event in his or her mind), a numbing of responsiveness and an avoidance of situations associated with the trauma, and a tendency to overreact to loud noises or quick movements (American Psychiatric Association, 1994). Among those at risk for PTSD are political refugees; torture victims; combat veterans; and survivors of rape, incest, alcoholic families, assault, domestic violence, war, and natural disasters (Bedics, Rappe, & Rappe, 1991).

THREE CAUSES OF TRAUMA

War

Children who witness acts of violence during war often have images that haunt them for years. The international development agency Save the Children (*Children at War*, 1994) estimated that 10 million children who are living today around the world have experienced emotional stress caused by war. Like children who are exposed to conventional warfare, young people in the United States who live under conditions of chronic violence (for example, in neighborhoods where gang warfare and police crackdowns are common) may experience symptoms of trauma (Masser, 1992). Parents, too, can become traumatized. Studies have found that parents everywhere who are unable to provide a safe environment for their children sometimes lose confidence and become emotionally unresponsive (*Starting Points*, 1994).

In addition, war often affects entire communities and nations. The collective trauma caused by the dropping of the atomic bombs on Hiroshima and Nagasaki still haunts Japan. And in the former Yugoslavia, symptoms of trauma are pervasive in communities that have been ravaged by war.

Migration

Since the mid-1970s, more people than ever before have been forced to flee their homes as a result of political repression, war, torture, and other violent conditions. For example, the number of refugees worldwide jumped from 10.5 million in 1984 to 14.5 million in 1994 (United Nations High Commission for Refugees, 1993, 1995). Not only are the situations that provoked flight horrific, but the actual process of migration can be filled with terrors as well. Among refugee populations who have been uprooted from their homes, PTSD is common (Prigoff, 1995). Many refugees experience a profound sense of loss or defeat as a result of being separated from "all that is important and familiar: family, friends, language, culture" (Kahn, 1994, p. 21).

Homelessness

Conditions of poverty and deprivation are both physically and psychologically damaging. When people are unable to provide for their own basic needs and those of dependent family members, their sense of security is shattered. Homelessness, for example, deprives people of their right to security and is often traumatizing, especially for children (Prigoff, 1995). As Bassuk and Gallagher (1990) noted:

> Researchers have . . . reported that the majority of homeless children suffer from serious developmental, emotional, and learning problems. . . . For preschoolers, these five years span critical developmental stages. Extended trauma during this time may initiate a cycle of underachievement and emotional problems that cannot readily be reversed. (p. 32)

A survey conducted in 30 U.S. cities found that families with children account for 39 percent of the homeless population and that children

account for just over one-quarter of the homeless population (Waxman, 1994).

THE EFFECTS OF UNRESOLVED TRAUMA: ROADBLOCKS TO DEVELOPMENT

If left untreated, trauma may prevent individuals from moving forward and living their lives to their full potential. Long-term effects of unresolved trauma include PTSD, low self-esteem, depression, chemical dependence, and violent behavior (California NASW chapter Center, 1994). Some common responses of traumatized individuals are flight response, identification with the oppressor, and truncated moral development.

Flight Response

Sometimes trauma evokes responses that initially function as a form of self-protection. The flight response, for example, involves the avoidance of painful memories; the trauma is hidden and denied as a defense against shame or self-blame (Figley, 1995; Herman, 1992). Denial prevents individuals from getting the help they need to address and cope with their current realities. In the absence of emotional healing, the protective response is likely to become rigid and chronic, resulting in self-defeating patterns of behavior (California NASW chapter Center, 1994).

Identification with the Aggressor

Traumatized individuals often suffer devastating assaults to self-esteem and increased helplessness and dependence as a result of their inability to protect themselves. Unless their trust is restored through psychological healing, they may adopt the dominators' perspective of themselves, forming a "traumatic bond" with their oppressors and internalizing or redirecting their aggression toward others who are similar to them (Dutton & Painter, 1993).

Role reversal, in which a former powerless victim assumes the attributes of the aggressor, is a critical dynamic in the cycle of violence. The former victim may provoke repeated abuse or reverse the roles, so the victim becomes the victimizer. Such learned and repeated patterns of behavior have been documented in cases of family violence, as well as physical assaults with deadly weapons (California NASW chapter Center, 1994). Violent acts—which may first seem to be irrational when considered as isolated incidents—are often understandable as the symptoms of painful, humiliating, and shameful experiences of violence from which the victims have not recovered (Kordon & Edelman, 1986).

Truncated Moral Development

Chronic violence has been linked to truncated moral development in several cases. Fields's (1987) research in Northern Ireland and the Middle East, for example, revealed that children who live in violent communities remain at more primitive stages of moral development than do other children. If adults, such as parents and teachers, do not model higher moral reasoning, then it is likely that moral development will not occur.

TOWARD SOLUTION: APPROACHES TO HEALING

Empowerment

Empowerment approaches to treating trauma, including self-help groups and community-based services, allow individuals, families, and communities to make peace with the past and to regain control of their lives. Victims can be empowered by developing trust, speaking the truth, and expressing grief.

Developing trust. Confidentiality and a safe, caring environment are essential to help trauma victims search for forgotten and unhappy memories and to rediscover a sense of their own power. Traumatized people often find it easier to share their feelings in a self-help group in which other members have had similar experiences (Prigoff, 1993).

Speaking the truth. The full disclosure of available facts about a traumatizing event and associated feelings is crucial for recovery. If disclosed, feelings of anxiety, powerlessness, pain, and fear are likely to be defused and diminished over time and to become part of a conscious life history and the development of identity (Prigoff, 1993).

Expressing grief. Grieving and accepting losses—of other people, of trust, of safety, and of the meaning of life—are critical components of psychic healing (California NASW chapter Center, 1994). In the global South, communities use unique interventions to encourage people to come to terms with their grief. These interventions may be based on cultural rituals and traditions, ceremonies, spiritual experiences, drama, dance, storytelling, artwork, music, and other group activities (Prigoff, 1995).

Community Cooperation

Because the healing process requires social supports and connectedness to others, it can be powerful when communities draw on their own resources to heal from violence and trauma (Poole, 1993; Prigoff, 1995). Here are two examples:

El Salvador. In a closed refugee camp in El Salvador, members divided responsibilities for child care, agriculture, food preparation, sewing, and carpentry so that everyone contributed to the survival and well-being of the community. New arrivals were assigned integral roles in the settlement to make them feel at home. Salvadoran psychologists who worked with this camp reported significant positive psychosocial results (Roe, 1992).

United States. Residents of five underdeveloped neighborhoods in Kansas City are working to rebuild their communities by offering support to one another. "Block leaders" receive limited financial compensation to spend time with young people and their parents, offering such services as help with homework, field trips, wake-up calls, home visits, and advocacy at school. They are demonstrating that neighbors can reduce crime and repair the fabric of their own communities, block by block (Pittman, 1995).

Apology and Forgiveness

Apologies by people or nations that have caused trauma to others are an important and powerful step on the path to healing (Kahn, 1994). When former South African president F. W. de Klerk offered a deep and dramatic apology for apartheid in April 1993, he helped pave the way for a future for South Africa. Similarly, former Governor of Alabama George Wallace accomplished what the United States as a nation has not yet achieved. Once an avowed segregationist who ordered dogs and fire hoses to be turned on African American civil rights demonstrators, he eventually came to the realization that he was wrong and publicly apologized for his former position. In 1982, he ran for a fourth term. In a dramatic testament to generosity and forgiveness, it was the African American vote that carried him (Lehigh, 1995).

Researchers view interpersonal forgiveness as the smallest unit of peacemaking. Moreover, forgiveness is coming to be seen as a legitimate method of international conflict resolution (personal correspondence with Beverly Flanigan, coordinator, National Conference on Forgiveness, School of Social Work, University of Wisconsin-Madison, April 27, 1995). Whether between individuals, groups, or nations, apologies for former wrongs (in tandem with a conciliatory forgiver) tend to soften the memory of former conflict and to promote an atmosphere from which mending and progress can occur (Kahn, 1994).

Conscientiousness and Democracy Building

For oppressed peoples, an important part of the healing process is their ability to analyze the political and social forces that contributed to their trauma in the first place and then to take action to end inequality. This kind of self-awareness and participation is essential for a true and flourishing democracy, liberty, and self-determination (Prigoff, 1993).

Real change and healing may mandate a shift in the traditional power structures of the past, enabling victims to gain more control over their lives and ensuring that atrocities are not repeated. Combatting helplessness at all levels and replacing it with hope and action for a better future are key elements in the complete recovery from trauma.

One inspiring story of the power of individuals to effect change comes from Guatemala. Motivated by the "disappearance" of their loved ones by government security forces, surviving relatives united to form El GAM—the Mutual Support Group for Relatives of the Disappeared. The founders had met by chance while looking for their sons and husbands in prisons and morgues. They exchanged names, phone numbers, and support. At the first official meeting in 1985, 25 women came together. One member recalled, "We all got up and told our personal stories. It was very emotional" (Guatemala, 1985, p. 10).

Subsequently, they petitioned and demonstrated in the streets, demanding to know what had happened to their family members. As the disappearances continued, the membership in El GAM swelled to nearly 1,000. For their courageous and selfless efforts to gain justice in the face of adversity, they have received international recognition and support. Today, they continue to work for democracy, justice, and human rights. Their leader and one of the original founders, Nineth Montenegro de García, was recently elected to the Guatemalan Parliament under a new, progressive political party comprised of a wide range of organizations that work for social justice and human rights (PBI/USA Report, 1996).

CASE STUDIES

The first case study illustrates the impact of trauma on one person. The other four case studies illustrate the different ways that people throughout the world are healing from violence-related trauma.

CASE STUDY 1
Initial Interview with H

H grew up in a small town in Cambodia where he led a happy and secure life with his parents, four sisters, and two brothers. When Pol Pot came to power, one of his sisters and his father were killed. His mother died of sickness a few months later. H was forced to separate from his siblings, whom he never heard from again. He was forced to labor long hours without food. He became emaciated, although he did not suffer any specific injuries. H remembered seeing people killed routinely and corpses being "piled up." In 1977, H escaped to Thailand, where he was a refugee for two years before he came to the United States at age 15.

After a three-year period of adjustment in the United States, H was referred to a school social worker because his grades were dropping owing to his inability to concentrate and sit still in class and because he was absent a great deal from school. When he was interviewed by the social worker, he became angry and irritable when asked about his feelings. Then he reluctantly said that he felt sad most of the time. When asked what his life had been like since he left Cambodia, H seemed close to tears. He said he had no trouble thinking about Cambodia, but he had never discussed what had happened there. He seemed angry and looked away when he described some early events.

H said that when people were killed, they were dumped in a mass grave and that he witnessed these killings every day for a while. He also said that he sometimes remembered traumatic events when he did not want to; for example, the Fourth of July fireworks brought back the memory of his father being shot. Throughout the interview, H seemed agitated and tapped his foot on the floor. (Adapted from Van Soest, 1992, p. 83)

CASE STUDY 2
The Circle of Healing

Aboriginal people in Manitoba, Canada, are using the Circle of Healing to address the problem of violence in their communities (MATCH International Centre, 1994). The circle was started by five or six women from the Hollow Water Reserve who began meeting secretly to share their problems and later opened their discussions to the community. The group connected the psychological, emotional, and physical violence they were subjected to with the economic, social, and political underdevelopment of their community. They realized that unless violence was dealt with, their community could not move forward. In 1987, the group decided to tackle sexual abuse directly when two rapists returned to the reserve after spending three years in jail and raped again. The people of the reserve turned to the Circle of Healing, a method as old as native society.

The Circle of Healing involves treating the entire community to exorcise the pervasive illness of violence through the use of two treatment programs:

a five-day intensive therapy program and a 13-step process that takes two to five years. The circle insists that an offender must admit his or her responsibility before it gets involved, on the principle that until the victimizer is healed, there will be more victims.

A key to the circle's power of healing is a special gathering at which members of the community, the victim, the abuser, and family members come together to face the crime. First, the abuser has to acknowledge the crime publicly. Then members of the community tell the abuser how they feel about what happened and offer their support for healing. They also speak to the victim and the families involved.

The abuser is given a "healing contract" that sets out his or her punishment—usually community work—and arrangements are made to protect the victim. When the contract expires, a cleansing ceremony is held to symbolize the return of balance to the abuser, the family, and the community. At this point, healing is considered to be complete, and the crime is to be forgotten.

CASE STUDY 3
Ms. G

Ms. G is a 72-year-old widow who has congestive heart failure. She lives with her 50-year-old son, Mr. G, and his family, which consists of his second wife, age 35, and their three young children ages two, three, and five. Ms. G was born in a small, rural community in a Central American country but raised her seven children in an urban area. Her husband worked as a laborer, and it was a continuous struggle to provide the basic necessities for the family, which also included her husband's widowed mother. Ms. G stated that her religious faith and belief that her sons would one day be successful sustained her through the hard times. Since her husband died in 1985, she has lived with her second son.

For more than a decade, Ms. G's native country has been experiencing political upheaval; the regime in power has been fighting rebel forces. Ms. G's two younger sons and one of her grandchildren were killed in the fighting. Mr. G emigrated with his family to the United States in 1991, and Ms. G joined them later that year. She has had difficulty adjusting and complains to her son and daughter-in-law, whom she thinks should take better care of her. Ms. G lacks medical insurance, and her son has refused to arrange and pay for the oxygen tank that she needs.

When Ms. G recently fell in a store, gasping for breath, she was taken to a nearby hospital and treated. A social worker was called in to speak with Ms. G and her son. A nurse's aide interpreted for Ms. G and her son, and it was determined that Mr. G was afraid to pay for his mother's care because his wife would be angry that their children would then have to do without. Ms. G stated that although she believed her son should care for her, she had seen her husband, children, and grandchild all die and that it was her turn to die. The social worker contacted a local priest who spoke the native language of Mr. and Ms. G. He was able to convince the Gs that Ms. G's respiratory problems could be averted and asked Ms. G to come talk with him at the church about her sadness over her relatives' deaths. (Case study contributed by Linda Vinton, associate professor, School of Social Work, Florida State University, Tallahassee; used with permission)

CASE STUDY 4
A Program for Traumatized Mozambican Women and Children

A multifaceted program was developed in Zambia in an attempt to meet the psychosocial needs of Mozambican women and children who had experienced many horrors before fleeing their country. Women's clubs were organized to provide mutual aid and understanding among women who had experienced similar traumas and to strengthen the women's parenting and homemaking skills. A program was developed around groups of four or five women who were known to be people from whom others sought assistance. These women were given support and training to develop cocounseling models. A similar program was requested and established for men (Ressler, Tortorici, & Marcelino, 1993).

A pilot program was initiated to involve village children who had been traumatized in structured play. In addition, a clinic-based infant-stimulation program was organized to encourage mothers to play with and stimulate their children after it was observed that the mothers, especially those who had experienced trauma, were unresponsive to their children and that some children were withdrawn.

A school-based program was developed to train preschool and elementary school teachers to be more aware of the special needs of traumatized children and to promote a more caring and supportive classroom environment for the children. Age-appropriate activities for the children included songs, storytelling, role-plays, and group discussions and activities through which children could recall their experiences and feelings in a safe and supportive environment.

Another aspect of the program that the organizers considered to be important was the "sensitization" of agency workers, village leaders, and others to the special needs of traumatized individuals and the provision of assistance in resolving these individuals' difficulties (Ressler et al., 1993).

CASE STUDY 5
Learning to Cry in the Same Room

Nancy Baron, a clinical psychologist based in Boston, spent two years exploring ways in which psychology can be used to help war widows and children who have been displaced by civil strife in Sri Lanka. She began by helping a small nongovernmental organization that was working with war widows, most of whom were under age 30 and some of whom had up to eight children. Many of the displaced families had been in camps for up to four years. . . .

[Baron] realized that in Sri Lanka she was working with a society that does not give people an opportunity to express sadness . . . "The society tries to make people forget. We gave them an opportunity to explore their feelings." She started with a group of perhaps 30 war widows from the four ethnic factions affected by the fighting. She used art to overcome language barriers. "They drew an early childhood that was happy, a young adulthood that was happy and then the beginning of the trouble after the death of the husband. . . . The women were able to sit together and say that each group was responsible for killing each other's husbands. Everyone was crying, and they were able to hug each other."

One woman did not cry. She pointed to the scar on her face and said that her husband had stabbed her. She was relieved when he was killed. "The women empathized with her. They could talk about the experience" (Mann, 1994).

REFERENCES

American Psychiatric Association. (1994). *Diagnostic and statistical manual of mental disorders* (4th ed.). Washington, DC: Author.

Bassuk, E. L., & Gallagher, E. M. (1990). The impact of homelessness on children. In N. A. Boxill (Ed.), *Homeless children: The watchers and the waiters* (pp. 19–34). New York: Haworth Press.

Bedics, B. C., Rappe, P. T., & Rappe, L. O. (1991). Preparing BSW professionals for identifying and salvaging victims of post traumatic stress disorder. In B. Shank (Ed.), *B.S.W. education for practice: Reality and fantasy. Refereed papers from the ninth annual BPD Conference, Orlando, Florida* (pp. 94–100). St. Paul, MN: University of St. Thomas.

California NASW chapter Center on Trauma, Violence, and Development. (1994). [Report submitted to the Violence and Development Project]. Sacramento: Author.

Children at war. (1994). (Available from Save the Children, 52 Wilton Road, Westport, CT 06880; phone 203-221-4000)

Dutton, D. G., & Painter, S. (1993). Emotional attachments in abusive relationships: A test of traumatic bonding theory. *Violence and Victims, 8,* 105–120.

Fields, R. (1987, October 25). *Terrorized into terrorist: Sequelae of PTSD in young victims.* Paper presented at the meeting of the Society for Traumatic Stress Studies, New York City.

Figley, C. R. (1995). *Compassion fatigue: Secondary traumatic stress disorder—Theory, research and treatment.* New York: Brunner/Mazel.

Guatemala: The group for mutual support. (1985). New York: Americas Watch.

Herman, J. L. (1992). *Trauma and recovery.* New York: Basic Books.

Kahn, A. B. (1994, August 22). *Violence and social development between conflicting groups.* Unpublished manuscript, California NASW Center on Trauma, Violence, and Development, Sacramento.

Kordon, D. R., & Edelman, L. L. (1986). *Efectos psicologicos de la represion politica.* Buenos Aires: Sudamericana/Planeta.

Lehigh, S. (1995, July 16). The art of saying "I'm sorry." *Boston Globe,* pp. 65, 67.

Mann, J. (1994, August 10). Learning to cry in the same room. *Washington Post,* p. E15.

Masser, D. (1992). Psychological functioning of Central American refugee children. *Child Welfare, 71,* 439–456.

MATCH International Centre. (1994). The Circle of Healing: Aboriginal women organizing in Canada. In M. Davies (Ed.), *Women and violence: Realities and responses worldwide* (pp. 234–239). Atlantic Highlands, NJ: Zed Books.

PBI/USA Report. (1996, March). [Newsletter]. (Available from Peace Brigades International/ USA, 2642 College Avenue, Berkeley, CA 94704; phone 510-540-0749)

Pittman, K. (1995, May–June). Rebuilding community, block by block. *Youth Today,* p. 46.

Poole, W. (1993). *The heart of healing: Institute of Noetic Sciences.* Atlanta: Turner.

Prigoff, A. (1993). *Violence, trauma, loss and deprivation: Psychological wounds and processes of healing.* Paper presented at the 10th Annual North America-Nicaragua Health Colloquium, Managua.

Prigoff, A. (1995). *Healing and recovery from psychological trauma, with individuals, families and communities.* Unpublished manuscript, School of

Social Work, California State University, Sacramento.

Ressler, E. M., Tortorici, J., & Marcelino, A. (1993). *Children in war: A guide to the provision of services.* New York: UNICEF.

Roe, M. (1992). Displaced women in settings of continuing armed conflict. *Women and Therapy, 13*(1–2), 89–102.

Starting points: Meeting the needs of your youngest children (Report of the Carnegie Task Force on Meeting the Needs of Young Children). (1994, April). New York: Carnegie Corporation.

United Nations High Commission for Refugees. (1993). *The challenge of protection.* New York: United Nations.

United Nations High Commission for Refugees. (1995). *Populations of concern to UNHCR.* New York: United Nations.

Van Soest, D. (1992). *Incorporating peace and social justice into the social work curriculum.* Washington, DC: Office of Peace and International Affairs, National Association of Social Workers.

Waxman, L. (1994). *A status report on hunger and homelessness in America's cities.* Washington, DC: U.S. Conference of Mayors.

ADDITIONAL RESOURCES

Amnesty International, USA
322 Eighth Avenue
New York, NY 10001
Phone: 212-807-8400
 An organization that works for the release of all prisoners of conscience and an end to torture and executions.

Save the Children
52 Wilton Road
Westport, CT 06880
Phone: 203-221-4000
 An organization that works with child victims of war in more than 25 countries. It trains social workers to provide treatment for emotional distress and to conduct programs for families.

E

Efficiency argument, for raising status of women, 58

El GAM, Mutual Support Group for Relatives of the Disappeared, 116

Emotional injury. *See* Trauma

Entrepreneurial Development Institute (TEDI), 99

Equity argument, for raising status of women, 58

Ethnicity
 defined, 77
 ethnic groups defined, 77
 field practicum, **68–69**
 general objectives, **67**
 human behavior in the social environment, **67–68**
 research, **68**
 social welfare policy, **68**
 social work theory and practice, **68**

Ethnoviolence
 defined, 77–78
 development (connection to), 80–81
 global problem of, 79–80
 hate crimes, **70–71**, 78
 militarism's influence on, 80. *See also* Militarism
 nongovernmental organizations' role, 82
 Rwanda's history of, 80
 social and economic inequity (impact of), 80–81
 Sudan's interethnic war, 80
 sustainable human development as antidote to, 81–82
 unjust development and, 81
 U.S. and Soviet Union world link to, 80
 U.S. history of, 79–80

F

50 Years Is Enough, 44

Flight response, unresolved trauma and, 114

Foreign assistance (U.S.), 16, 36, 43

G

Gandhi, Mahatma, poverty characterization by, 35

García, Nineth Montenegro de, 116

Gender analysis (exercise), **52–53**

Gender-sensitive development, 59

Gender violence. *See* Women, violence against

Global Exchange, 6

Global issue, critical evaluation of the news media's coverage of a (writing assignment), **11**

Global South
 child development statistics of, 36–37
 defined, **6**, 15–16
 disaster relief (myths about), 43
 drug production/trafficking/consumption in, 18, 43–44, 96–98
 global South is where . . . (class discussion), **6–7**
 hate violence in (history of), 79
 health care access of, 36
 infant mortality, 17
 international development of (myths about), 42–44
 intertwined future with U.S., 18–19, 43–44. *See also* United States
 learning about links between the U.S. and a country in (writing assignment), **28–29**
 life expectancy, 17
 military expenditures, 18
 North–South poverty link summary, 38
 poverty rates, 35, 38
 relation to global North, **6**
 wealth disparity with global North, 35

Grameen Bank (Bangladesh), 18, **27**, 40

Grassroots economic alternatives (poverty), 39–41

Green Belt Movement, 39

H

H, trauma case study of, 116

Handbook on Accreditation Standards and Procedures (1994), **3**

Hate crimes. *See also* Ethnoviolence
 dynamics of youth, hate, and violence, **70–71**
 study results, **70–71**
 tailoring the response, **70**
 types of, 78

Health, poverty links to, 36

Hernandez, Angelica, case study of, 38

Holocaust denial groups, 79

Homelessness, as cause of trauma, 114

How does the world eat? (experiential classroom exercise), **27–28**

Human Development Report, 21
Hunger
    discussion of the myths about, **28**
    implications for social workers, 18–19
    myths about, **28**, 41–42
    Violence and Development Project and, 16
Hunger 1995: The Causes of Hunger, 21

I

Identification with the aggressor, traumatized victims and, 114–115
Immigrants. *See also* Ethnoviolence
    immigration/poverty relationship, 19, 38
    migration as cause of trauma, 114
    short lecture and quiz on (exercise), **71–74**
India,
    Kerala, India, family violence case study of, **51–52**, 60–61
    what one can learn from India case study (SEWA), **27**, 40–41
InterAction: American Council for Voluntary International Action, 20, 45
International Activities Committee Office of Peace and International Affairs, 20
International Center for Research on Women, gender-sensitive development recommendations, 59
International Council on Social Welfare, 45
International development
    myths about, 42–44
    test students' knowledge of (questions and answers), **7**
International development organizations. *See* Nongovernmental organizations (NGOs)
International Women's Year World Conference in Mexico City (1975), 55
Intervention plan, addressing family violence through (writing assignment), **52**

J

Julie, drug abuse case study of, **89**, 98–99

K

Kerala, India, family violence case study of, **51–52**, 60–61
Ku Klux Klan, **70**, 79

L

Learning about the refugees in your community (research assignment), **6**
Learning to cry in the same room, trauma case study of, 118–119
Linking family structure with violence and violence prevention in Kerala, India, **51–52**, 60–61

M

Male domination, gender violence and, 57
Medway, hate crime case study of, 78–79
Menchú, Rigoberto, 81
Microenterprise, concept of, 18
Mid-Decade World Conference for Women (Copenhagen, 1980), 55
Migration, as cause of trauma, 114. *See also* Immigrants
Militarism
    development resources drained by, 18, 80
    ethnoviolence fueled by, 80. *See also* Ethnoviolence
    gender violence and, 57
    trauma caused by, 113–114
Mission hate crimes, **70**, 78
Mozambican women and children, trauma case study of, **110–111**, 118
Ms. G, trauma case study of, **110**, 117–118
Myths
    about hunger, **28**, 41–42
    about international development and poverty, 42–44
    short lecture and quiz on dispelling, **28–30**

N

Narcotics. *See* Drug abuse
NASW. *See* National Association of Social Workers
National Association for the Advancement of Colored People, 82
National Association of Social Workers (NASW), *Social Workers and the Challenge of Violence Worldwide* (videotape), **5**
National Clearinghouse for Alcohol and Drug Information, 102
Nazi Skinhead movement, **70**, 79
Neve Shalom Kibbutz, Jewish–Arab bilingual school of, 82

Universal Declaration of Human Rights, 44
World Summit for Social Development
(Copenhagen), 44
United States
    battery to women in, 56
    cocaine use in, 95, 97
    development efforts needed in, 17
    foreign assistance (advantages and myths of),
        43
    foreign assistance budget, 16, 36
    health insurance availability in, 36
    history of ethnoviolence in, 79–80
    hunger in, **28**, 41
    infant mortality in, 17
    literacy survey, 17
    military expenditures, 18
    poverty in, 35, 37
    trade with poor countries (myths about), 43
    welfare budget (1995), 36
United States Committee for Refugees, 83
United Way, racial injustice and, 82
Universal Declaration of Human Rights (UN),
    44
Urbanization, as precipitant of violence, 58

V
Vignettes
    classroom discussion (trauma), **107–108**
    role-playing and discussion exercise (drug
        abuse), **89–91**
Violence (overview). *See also* Children, violence
        against; Drug abuse; Ethnoviolence;
        Poverty; Trauma; Women, violence against
    defined, 16–17
    effects of on development, 18
    effects of worldwide, 15
    field practicum, **5**
    general objectives, **3**
    human behavior in the social environment,
        4
    research, **5**
    social welfare policy, **4–5**
    social work theory and practice, **4**
    threats to personal security and social stability,
        16–17
Violence and Development Project, expanding
        definition of violence, 16

W
Wallace, George, 116
Wangari, Maathai, case study of, 39
War. *See* Militarism
Weasel and the Logan 30, drug abuse case study
        of, **89**, 98
What one can learn from India case study, **27**
White supremacist movement, 79
Women, violence against
    Annapurna Mahila Mandal case study, 61–62
    changing political and economic systems
        (effects of), 58
    developing an intervention plan to address
        (written assignment), **52**
    development that addresses, 59–60
    domestic violence, 57–58
    field practicum, **51**
    gender analysis (exercise), **52–53**
    gender-sensitive development, 59
    general objectives, **49**
    global problem of (statistics), 55–56
    human behavior in the social environment,
        49–50
    linking family structure with violence and vio-
        lence prevention case study, 60–61
    male domination, 57
    militarism and, 57
    1975 International Women's Year World
        Conference (Mexico City), 21
    1980 Mid-Decade World Conference for
        Women (Copenhagen), 21
    1985 World Conference on Women (Nairobi),
        21
    position paper on raising the status of women
        (writing assignment), **52**
    raising the status of women, 52, 58
    research, **50–51**
    social welfare policy, **50**
    social work theory and practice, **50**
    sustainable human development as antidote to,
        58–59
    underdevelopment as precipitant of, 58
    women healing from violence in Nicaragua
        case study, **51**, 60
    Women's Commission for Refugee Women and
        Children, 64
Working Women's Forum (Madras, India), 57

World. *See also* Global South; United Nations;
    United States
  development inequities in, 17–18
  global wealth disparity, 18–19, 35
  population/income breakdown, 16
  poverty rates, 35
World Conference on Women (Nairobi, 1985), 21
World Development Report, 21

World Military and Social Expenditures, 21
World Summit on Children, 19
World Summit for Social Development, 19
World-Watch Institute, violence against women,
    55

Y
Yunus, Muhammad, 18, 40

Dorothy Van Soest, DSW, is associate dean and associate professor at the School of Social Work, University of Texas at Austin. She has authored several articles and chapters on issues related to violence, peace, social justice, and development, as well as the book *Incorporating Peace and Social Justice into the Social Work Curriculum* (NASW, 1992). Her forthcoming book, *The Global Crisis of Violence: Common Problems, Universal Consequences, Shared Solutions*, will be published by the NASW Press in 1997. She is former director of the NASW Violence and Development Project.

Jane Crosby is director of the Violence and Development Project for the National Association of Social Workers. She received her master's of social work degree from Boston University in 1991. She previously worked at Oxfam America, an international development agency, where she directed the national education and fundraising hunger campaign, Fast for a World Harvest.

Cover and interior designed by Watermark Design.
Composed by Long-Run Publications
in Goudy and Univers.
Printed by Graphic Communications, Inc. on 60# Windsor Offset.